MAKE

HOLLYWOOD

GREAT AGAIN

★ ★ ★ ★ ★

CINEMA IN THE ERA OF PRESIDENT

TRUMP

BY: MICHAEL JOLLS

Praise for

THE FILMS OF
STEVEN SPIELBERG

By Michael Jolls

"The book examines in great detail the filmography of one of the most prolific filmmakers that has ever lived."

- **Adam C. Better,** *Amblin Road*

"Tells the story of a shattered childhood relentlessly paved with cinematic triumphs."

- **Sardonic,** *@Sardonica*

"*The Films of Steven Spielberg* is packed so full of information in such a quick read, that unlike *Jaws*, you won't need a bigger boat… or a longer book."

- **Kris Galvan,** *@parkedinfrontofthescreen*

"Michael Jolls really displays his love for film, as well as his love for the great and unforgettable directors that we've had over the years, as he takes us on a journey through Steven Spielberg's tragic childhood, all the way to his rise to the legendary filmmaker we know today, as well as make the reader gain even more of an appreciation for Steven Spielberg's genius films."

- *2 Awesome Men*, **YouTube Channel**

"Michael Jolls is able to capture the importance of reoccurring themes through his work through the use of technically astute terminology that will provide film students with plenty of informative views. Jolls utilizes Spielberg's chronological filmography to distinctly split them into separate important chapters into a pseudo-autobiographical book, that also has a personal undertone. He clearly is inspired by Spielberg's work, not just as a director, but as an artist who upholds the utmost of integrity. The book isn't a shrine, it's not filled with consistent compliments. It's a journey. A bewildering study of a master and his legacy where we explore directing techniques, screenplays and casting choices. What more could one ask for? Highly recommended for film buffs, students and those who are just fascinated by a man that shaped cinema."

- **Luke Andrews, *The Media Diorama***

"A fantastic and interesting read!"

- **Alex Fernandes, *@Movie_Geek98***

"Once you start reading it, it is hard to put it down. 5/5."

- **Aakanksha Jain, *Books Charming***

"An interesting introduction to Spielberg's background, interests, motivations, and collaborations."

- **Heather L. Barksdale, *Heather's Bookshelf***

"The similarities Jolls talks about in *Schindler's List*, *Amistad* and *Lincoln* gave a fresh perspective to the movies… If you are a fan of Spielberg movies or would love to enlighten yourself about this amazing director's works, you should definitely read this book!"

- **Christeena Thomas, *@the_laconic_reader***

"I was impressed with the depth of the research into this man, his life, and the films he produced."

- **Storeybook Reviews**

MAKE
HOLLYWOOD
GREAT AGAIN

★ ★ ★ ★ ★

CINEMA IN THE ERA OF PRESIDENT
TRUMP

BY: MICHAEL JOLLS

Released, May 2020
Update, April 2022

ISBN-13: 9798634377155

Table of Contents

Introduction

"My God, the fun."

— Tom Hanks as Ben Bradlee, *The Post*

We all know the story. On June 16, 2015, Donald J. Trump announced his candidacy for the following year's presidential election. He was one of the most *popular* names and one of the most *unlikely* victors.

I believed that by the following spring, Trump would commit political suicide by doing something so outlandish that would cost him the nomination (anyone remember Howard Dean's "yeeaaahhwwww" in early 2004?)

However, by late summer 2016, the American political story was more captivating than it had been in a long time.

I don't mean to discard the controversial 2000 election between George W. Bush and Al Gore, but that was over a decade ago and part of the pre-9/11 era. The 2004 election had intriguing moments (which are particularly fascinating in hindsight), but sadly we tend to overlook that election. The landmark election of Barack Obama in November 2008 was moving and inspirational, although his victory was predictable months in advance. The 2012 election was, in my opinion, premature, as the key criticisms of the Obama administration hadn't yet come to fruition. Additionally, the candidates of all these elections (John Kerry, John McCain, Mitt Romey) were not as dynamic as the figures of Hillary Clinton and Donald Trump.

In 2016, you had two candidates that both shared household name status for at least the previous 20 years. You had more "October surprises" than ever before with deleted emails, raunchy audiotapes, and rape accusations.

Let's take a moment and consider the popular catch-phrases of past elections: in 2004, John Kerry was tagged with the *Flipper* theme song because he kept changing his stance on key issues. In the 2008 election, Obama wrapped up the country in the spirit of "Hope & Change," with occasional references to "Joe the Plumber." The 2012 election was perfectly summed up by a friend of mine's Halloween costume: he showed up to a party dressed as Mitt Romney with a plush Big Bird doll hanging from a noose and a binder with "Women" scrolled on the cover in big black Sharpie (referencing the debates when Romney talked about cutting funding for PBS and referenced "binders full of women" ready for employment).

As for the 2016 election? Take your pick: "Make America Great Again," "I'm With Her," "Lock Her Up," "[Basket of] Deplorables," "Drain the Swamp," "Grab em' by the Pussy" and "Nasty Woman". Hell, even "Feel the Bern" became a common catchphrase, and Bernie Sanders didn't even make the November ballot!

It'll be at least a hundred years or so before history tells us which of these elections were the most consequential to the "American story," yet without a doubt, the 2016 election changed the contemporary culture's vernacular. If events played out as the vast majority of the planet expected and Hillary Clinton was elected president, would the last three and a half years have continued to fixate our attention? I'm not sure. Nevertheless, the political history that played out in the aftermath has been downright **outrageous.**

Again, poor Howard "yeeaaahhwwww" Dean from 2004 sorta pales in comparison, right?

***

I don't watch movies actively looking for the political agenda, rather the correlation between cinema and politics has always been something my brain automatically gets attuned to if I sense it.

We are always encouraged to read and/or watch older "stuff" in the context of when it debuted. I can't help watching a film that's decades old, and not think of the events from that era and how the movie has "aged" with regards to the present day. The grandiose subject of World War II offers countless perspectives from which we could study that period of history. Consider the different World War II dramas we've seen over the last eighty years: *Casablanca* (1942); *The Great Escape* (1963); *Schindler's List* (1993); and *Dunkirk* (2017). Out of these four titles, the themes, the settings, the tones, the music and the very narratives of these respective films are different – despite addressing the same subject. Each of those four films, two fiction and two non-fiction, are somewhat exclusive to the era of when they were produced. We can go through any given decade of cinema and cherry pick a dozen or so World War II films, and each would grant us a little insight to a cultural or sociological topic of the era.[1]

***

The other reason why I get fixated on the "message" of a particular film is from my own experience behind the camera. The productions that were the most enjoyable to shoot and edit were the ones where I had an "agenda" throughout the production. That doesn't mean they were my best works. Rather, a simple 2 minute comedy bit could be cathartic because I was working out something that was irritating me. (If you're questioning this, ask a stand-up comedian where he or she gets their material from. I'm willing to bet some of it comes from a source of frustration). It's unthinkable that a movie studio would pour millions into a production without it serving a purpose or agenda of some kind. I promise you, even the bawdiest comedy has some axe to grind on a subliminal level.

Looking at the predominantly liberal Hollywood, it was safe to assume that the vast majority of the films that released after the election of 2016 were going to wrestle with the unimaginable tenant in the White House. Because Donald Trump has remained such a polarizing figure, the issues surrounding him get heightened. The emotions get stronger. The rhetoric becomes more energetic.

Putting Our Discussion Into Perspective

From the outset, I intended *Make Hollywood Great Again* to try and remain "booklet" length. A thorough 200-odd-page book on the cinema of the late 2010s is for a better writer to do somewhere down the road. We need to put a little mileage from "now" before we can authentically assess the collective films we've been watching.

The intended audience for *Make Hollywood Great Again* are the film students. (If you are not in film school or don't produce videos, don't worry. This book won't go off on tangents about frame-rates or optic lens ratios). One of my regrets about the time I spent in formal "college film education" was that I ignored the political events around me and found myself playing catch-up years later. I wouldn't want to discourage film students from their studies, but it's also unhealthy to be ignorant of events happening in the contemporary world. (Also, I'm not naive enough to think that "art" professors aren't spending an average 4 minutes of every single class reiterating the "Trump is *literally* Hitler" rant. You're in Film Editing-101 to learn a trade, not your professor's political agenda).

There are three rules I choose to adhere to with regards to this retrospective:

Rule 1: We Can't Cover Everything

It's too easy to wander off into any given "talking point" from the last couple years. As much as I would have liked to address "The Squad" (the four freshmen congresswomen), or Russian collusion, I decided to only address topics that Hollywood championed via the films released between 2017 and early 2020. Just because *Dark Waters* is about a mass illness, it doesn't mean we're going to force the issue of coronavirus into the conversation.

Granted, it might seem odd that I did not privilege some presumably obvious titles, such as *Beatriz at Dinner*; *Booksmart*; *Knives Out* or *Unplanned*. For any number of reasons, those films didn't offer the subtext that warranted a larger conversation at this point in time. To properly explore them would have made this book a little too long, and like fine wine, some will make for better conversation after they age a little.

Rule 2: Being Mindful of Themes that
Hollywood Addressed Prior to January 2017

It's important to remember that just because Donald Trump (surprisingly) became president, that doesn't mean that the film industry suddenly shifted gears and every single movie released after November 8, 2016 had a newfound "Trump" agenda.

Obviously, some films released during President Trump's first term were a direct response to his presidency; the documentaries *Death of a Nation* (2018) and *Fahrenheit 11/9* (2018) would be the most obvious examples of this. However, the vast majority of movies released in 2017, and 2018 could have been in anywhere from developmental stages to post-production when Trump was sworn in, let alone the presumptive Republican nominee. This means that if we examine themes *only* through the prism of "when Trump was president," our view will become distorted. For example, if we look at *Detroit* (2017) or *Green Book* (2018) strictly under the pretense of that it released when Trump was president, then we risk ignoring the first half of the 2010s which showcased a number of moderately successful movies about the Civil Rights issues including *The Help* (2011); *42* (2013); *Fruitvale Station* (2013); *The Butler* (2013); *Selma* (2014); *Fences* (2016) and *Hidden Figures* (2016).

On the flip side, we're also not going to highlight films that prefigured a Trumpesque figure. Yes, there is a conversation to be had about Julianne Moore's depiction of Sarah Palin in the made-for-TV *Game Change* (2012), or the development of Kevin Spacey's character in the TV series *House of Cards* (2013-2018), or the joy of greed shown through Leonardo DiCaprio in *The Wolf of Wall Street* (2013). Again, we're not going to cover everything.

Rule 3: Relevant vs. Irrelevant

Alright, this gets a little tricky, especially if you're an annoying, self-proclaimed expert, quick to throw a temper tantrum if/when your "fan theory" doesn't work.

We really *should not* discredit parallels that the collective "audience" has already made. The best example of this comes by way of Josh Brolin's Thanos from *Avengers: Infinity War* (2018), specifically the term, "orange Thanos." Countless fans and critics, myself included, saw parallels between Donald Trump and the headline villain of the Marvel Cinematic Universe (MCU). No doubt that the publicity stunt of Brolin reading Trump's tweets in his Thanos voice on *The Late Show with Stephen Colbert* helped fuel this concept.(2)

However (one would hope the film nerds realized this), Marvel Studios had previously invested too much time and energy into the complete MCU narrative for them to have radically fixated the last couple of films to be about Trump. The first installment of the MCU, *Iron Man*, was released in May 2008 when George W. Bush was still president. The character of Thanos was first teased in *Avengers* in May 2012. Josh Brolin made his formal appearance as Thanos in *Guardians of the Galaxy* in August 2014, the summer before Trump even announced his candidacy for president.

Due to the popularity of the MCU, the outspoken liberal politics many of the stars adhere to (Don Cheadle, Chris Evans, Scarlett Johansson and Mark Ruffalo), the way President Trump's critics played into the "orange Thanos" concept, and the Official Trump Campaign's own version of Thanos from *Avengers: Endgame* (2019), the concept deserves acknowledgement.(3)

However, if we were really going to roll up our sleeves and dig into the full Thanos vs. Trump comparison, it requires a whole assessment of the comic book genre. Comic book characters are often adapted and customized to fit the era of their popularity. The Iron Man and Hulk comics were heavily inspired by the 1960s Cold War era nuclear and... do you see how LONG this book could get?

Bottom line, a discussion of how the MCU reflects current politics is a topic unto itself, and that's a book for a better author to write. Let's not even get started on *Joker* (2019).

Obviously, we could easily drag out this discussion to include 20 or 25 films. However, there comes a point when the conversation becomes self-gratuitous, nonsensical and an inevitable pile of "stuff." Furthermore, as of this writing, Trump's still in office and we don't know if he'll be around for a second term - so why try and write the definitive retrospective when it's not even over yet? For example, some saw connections between Trump and a handful of the 2017 films, however those parallels were either dismissed or were said to be unintentional. This muddles our ability to have honest analysis. There comes a point when we can read *too* much into things. For example, just because Supreme Leader Snoke (Andy Serkis) has a golden robe in *Star Wars: Episode VIII: The Last Jedi* (2017), that doesn't mean it was a nod to Trump and his villainous reign over the galax… err, I mean, the United States.(4) Or it doesn't mean that the military in *Jurassic World: Fallen Kingdom* (2018) is an allegory to unrestricted funding of the GOP, and the dinosaurs are all Mexicans. Or, just because Trump likes Elton John's music and called Kim Jong Un, "rocketman," that doesn't mean we need to carefully study the musical, *Rocketman* (2019) for hidden messages to North Korea. Or, we don't need to view Vera Farmiga's character in *Godzilla: King of the Monsters* (2019) as a symbolic Alexandria Ocasio-Cortez, turned environmental terrorist.

If you're rolling your eyes reading the above, then you get the point.

In the case of the films we've highlighted, the filmmakers *admitted* that they were conscious of the Trump presidency and the political climate throughout the production. Additionally, despite the political agendas of these films, there is something to be learned from watching them regardless of political leaning. Each of these films, for better or worse, have elements that are worthwhile contributions to the political conversation.

My Own Bias

It's very important that you, the reader, know where I'm coming from. I personally get distracted when reading film academia and the topic of politics comes up because I'm too busy second guessing the author's beliefs. Also, you've made it this far and hopefully you can tell I'm not a fanatic. I'm not a white supremacist, sitting here wearing a MAGA hat, stroking my AR-15 as I type... or a feckless Social Justice Warrior, wearing a pink Pussyhat and keeping a tab open to my Twitter feed because I feel compelled to troll a bigot about cisgender koala bears.

I consider myself a conservative who actively seeks a moderate standpoint. I find myself agreeing with most Republican policies, but that doesn't mean I believe Democratic policies are wrong or should be totally discarded. While I am more willing to support a "right wing" cause, I won't outright dismiss a "left wing" petition. Actually, I'm grateful for those on the left, who take the initiative to champion good causes that don't necessarily excite me. Go green? I don't care, but I'm not going to oppose being more environmentally friendly. I drive a hybrid primarily to save on gas, but I'm happy to know I'm cutting back on exhaust fumes. The mass shootings? I blame the person, mental health and dangerous ideologies before guns, however I'm not going to oppose stricter background checks. Black lives matter? Yes. Blue lives matter? Yes. Ultimately, I'm more of an "All Lives Matter" mindset. We could go through the issues one by one, and you would find that I'm a fairly agreeable person with exception to fanatics.

I did not like and wrote off Donald Trump for months, however I came around to strongly supporting him in 2016 and thus far haven't had a reason to cease my support... duck! ***SMASH-CRASH!***

Did you just hear your far-left professor chuck this little booklet across the room? If my support for President Trump *infuriates* you, just know I'm laughing at you. The same way I'm laughing at the right-wing lunatic who didn't even get this far because he or she won't even touch the book. The word

"Hollywood" is on the cover, so they just snarled at it on the bookshelf.

True story: in the months leading up to this book's releasing, at least a half dozen conspiracy theory wackos saw the cover online and thought this was Hollywood's attempt to destroy the Trump campaign. Who said don't judge a book by its cover? Please keep it up! I revel at people getting triggered over nonsense. (I don't do well with close minded people if you couldn't already tell).

I have read most of the top-selling political books from the last three years, *both* the conservative and the liberals ones; you can review my "Political Bibliography" in the back, which lists the books I've read so you can judge my balanced diet of reading material. I strive to be aware of what each side says. To be honest, I find there's a lot more middle ground than you would think, but since the media prefers American politics to be one big WWE-wrestling match… *sigh.*

A lot of time is wasted in pointless arguments.

I want to make it very clear that my political beliefs will be separated from the film analysis presented. This booklet is primarily a work of observation, education and analysis; my own opinions come second. I end each of these pseudo-essays with my own take, under the heading "Final Verdict," thereby restricting my own bias and keeping it outside of the formal lecture. (Yes, I realize the whole damn book is my opinion *however*, hopefully you'll learn something regardless if our politics clash or not).

At the end of the day, this is a pseudo "film lecture" on a topic that I've enjoyed watching unfold in the public forum since 2016. Whether you've been thrilled or horrified by the events of the times, I hope you will find this discussion educational and that it will enrich your film viewing experiences regardless of your political sway.

Before We Begin...

This book is best suited for a reader familiar with the movies listed below. Nevertheless, we'll strive to be as articulate as possible. (Sometimes pre-reading about a film before you watch it can enhance the viewing experience!) Please be advised that "spoilers" are openly discussed:

The Post (2017, Steven Spielberg)
Blackkklansman (2018, Spike Lee)
The Front Runner (2018, Jason Reitman)
Dark Waters (2019, Todd Haynes)
Richard Jewell (2019, Clint Eastwood)
The Hunt (2020, Craig Zobel)

In addition, both *The Birth of a Nation* (1915, D.W. Griffith) and *All the President's Men* (1976, Alan J. Pakula) are referenced throughout.

Since most of these films are based off true events and actual people, I have made a strong effort to differentiate between **actor** and **character**.

Also, don't hesitate to take your time with this booklet. If it's been a while since you saw one of these films, throw it on in the background while you do laundry, or take 10 or 15 minutes to re-watch clips or behind-the-scenes on YouTube to refresh yourself.

Chapter 1

The Post

The Integrity of Journalism

"This [*The Post*] to me is a patriotic movie and I don't think it's a partisan film. I didn't make this as a Democrat. I made this as a believer in a free press, in our first amendment rights, as a believer in journalism and also, as a bit of an antidote for this horrible term that makes us wonder what is true and what is false, and that term is 'fake news.'"[1]

— Steven Spielberg, November 2017

Although Spielberg stated that he would have directed *The Post* had Hillary Clinton won the 2016 election,[2] the film was initially perceived to be a rallying cry for the protection of the First Amendment, and a rebuttal to President Trump's lambasting of the media's bias towards him. The vast majority of the country is at least subliminally aware that the mainstream media has a liberal bent. The recurring critiques of Republicans and President Trump on CNN or ABC, the heavy attacks by MSNBC and the doomsday headlines of *The New York Times* really shouldn't surprise anyone. Furthermore, the concept of "liberal Hollywood" is part of America's cultural makeup; society anticipates Hollywood to be liberal the same way society anticipates Christians to be conservative. Yes, there are dozens of exceptions, but for the last couple of decades the trends have remained the same. With this in mind, the combination of Steven Spielberg, Tom Hanks and Meryl Streep — three of the biggest names in the last forty years of showbiz and openly supportive of the Democratic party — the political intentions of *The Post* were crystal clear.

The Relationship Between
Steven Spielberg & Donald Trump

Trump makes two references to Spielberg in his famous book, *The Art of the Deal* – first stating that Spielberg belongs in the category of successful business people who understand their market. Secondly, in Trump's own showboating manner, he names Spielberg in a list of celebrities that have an apartment in Trump Tower, New York. (The apartment was apparently purchased for him by Universal Studios, although this is unconfirmed).

Throughout the 1990s, both Trump and Spielberg shared an open friendliness with the Clintons. Ironically, in the year 2000, Spielberg offered his Trump Tower apartment to Hillary Clinton to use as a crash pad during her New York Senatorial race. During the mid-2000s, both Spielberg and Trump expressed irritation with the W. Bush administration, specifically the war in Iraq. In late November 2012, Donald Trump tweeted, "Steven Spielberg is a great filmmaker. Go see 'Lincoln.'" In April 2015, Trump tweeted a picture of himself and Spielberg as a "Throwback Thursday" photo.

Clearly the 2016 election would alter their friendship as Spielberg and his wife Kate Capshaw reportedly donated a joint $2.3 million to Hillary Clinton's campaign. Nevertheless, in January 2018, the White House requested a copy of *The Post* to screen in the Family Theatre. The request was granted, although when and to whom it was screened remains in question.

The Politics of Tom Hanks & Meryl Streep

In May 2008, Tom Hanks announced his support for Barack Obama's candidacy, and eight months later (January 2009) he gave a short speech honoring Abraham Lincoln at the star-studded inauguration celebration. During the 2016 election cycle, Hanks supported Hillary Clinton with pithy remarks that also disparaged Trump in a variety of press interviews. Before leaving office, President Obama awarded Hanks the Presidential Medal of Freedom in mid-November 2016.

With regards to Meryl Streep, it's worth noting that in 1967, her then boyfriend, a Vietnam veteran by the name of Mike Booth, went to protest President Richard Nixon at Morristown, New Jersey. When Nixon was leaving the event, Booth was accidentally propelled forward due to the hysteria of the crowd, landing feet in front of Nixon. He proceeded to scream in the president's face. Moments after Nixon departed, Booth was detained by Secret Service and interrogated. Although there is no record of how Streep reacted to this story, it's safe to assume she shared (at least partially) the same disapproval of Nixon that her then boyfriend had.[3]

Jumping ahead to the modern era, Streep would earn the Kennedy Center Honor in 2011, awarded to her by President Obama. Then again in 2014, Obama would also present Streep with the Presidential Medal of Freedom, where the two bestowed praise upon each other.

Meryl Streep's Golden Globes Speech

Throughout his campaign in 2015, Trump periodically claimed that thousands of people were cheering in New Jersey when the World Trade Center towers collapsed on 9/11. In late November 2015, this claim was questioned and the Trump campaign referred to a *Washington Post* article, co-written by Serge F. Kovaleski, as proof that Muslims were celebrating the fall of the Twin Towers. The article stated that:

> law enforcement detained and questioned a number of people who were allegedly seen celebrating the attacks and holding tailgate-style parties on rooftops while they watched the devastation.[4]

Kovaleski issued a statement in response to the Trump campaign saying, "I certainly do not remember anyone saying that thousands, or even hundreds of people were celebrating. That was not the case, as best as I can remember."

At a Trump Rally the following day, Donald Trump brought up Kovaleski's statement. Although he never said his name, Trump said, "...written by a nice reporter, now the poor guy, you gotta see this guy..." He then bent his wrists and flailed his arms:

> 'Uhh, I don't know what I said. Uhh, I don't remember!' He's going like, 'I don't remember. Maybe that's what I said.' This is fourteen years ago - he's still! They didn't do a retraction! Fourteen years ago - they did no retraction![5]

By the following morning, the incident drew widespread criticism as it appeared that Trump mocked Kovaleski's arthrogryposis, a disability that resulted in joint contracture of his right arm and hand. Following the media's condemnation, Trump said that he was not mocking Kovaleski's disability because he did not know what Kovaleski looked like. Yet, Kovaleski had said that while reporting on Trump for the *New York Daily News,* the two had been on a first-name basis and had met face-to-face on dozens of occasions since the late 1980s. The fact that the two knew each other was also corroborated by multiple witnesses.

***

A little over a year later, in January 2017, Streep gave a scathing denunciation of, by then President-Elect Trump, at the Golden Globe Awards when winning the Cecil B. DeMille award. Streep said:

> An actor's only job is to enter the lives of people who are different from us and let you [the audience] feel what that feels like, and there were many, many, many powerful performances this year that did exactly that. Breathtaking passionate work. But there was one performance this year that stunned me. It sank its hooks in my heart. Not because it was good; it was — there was nothing good about it. But it was effective and it did its job. It made its intended audience laugh, and show their teeth. It was that moment when the person asking to sit in the most respected seat in our country imitated a disabled reporter. Someone he outranked in privilege, power and the capacity to fight back. It, it kind of broke my heart when I saw it, and I still can't get it out of my

head, because it wasn't in a movie. It was real life. And
this instinct to humiliate, when it's modeled by someone
in the public platform, by someone powerful, it filters
down into everybody's life, because it kinda gives
permission for other people to do the same thing.
Disrespect invites disrespect, violence incites violence.
And when the powerful use their position to bully others
we all lose.(6)

The speech, particularly the denunciation of Trump, was
instantly championed by Hollywood, Democrats and the liberal
media. Trump responded on Twitter the next day, saying:

Meryl Streep, one of the most over-rated actresses in
Hollywood, doesn't know me but attacked last night at
the Golden Globes. She is a Hillary flunky who lost big.
For the 100th time, I never "mocked" a disabled reporter
(would never do that) but simply showed him
"groveling" when he changed a 16 year old story that he
had written in order to make me look bad. Just more very
dishonest media!(7)

***

Hollywood wasted no time. In early March 2017, just two
months after Streep's speech, a new project called *The Pentagon
Papers* went into production touting the household names of
Spielberg, Hanks and Streep, along with a co-screenwriter of 2015's
Best Picture winner, *Spotlight*.

As with Spielberg's *Catch Me If You Can* (2002) and
Munich (2005), *The Post* would fly from pre-production to movie
theatres in less than a year.(8)

Spielberg's Authorship in *The Post*

Spielberg's historical pieces have a tendency to
circumnavigate history with a small, yet an all-encompassing story.

The vantage point of *Schindler's List* is that of a
businessman played by Liam Neeson with influential Nazi
affiliates, who in the process of making money off the war effort,
goes through personal moral convictions about the segregation and

mass murder of a single race. The drama teeters on two characters, a humble Jewish accountant and a psychopathic SS kommandant flanking Liam Neeson's character. Additionally, *Schindler's List* functions like a kaleidoscope, showing the audience a variety of Jews suffering at the hands of the Nazis. This combination: Neeson's moral dilemma, the conflicting nature of his two key business associates, and the sporadic intermixing of victims, allows *Schindler's List* to showcase the full emotional gravitas of the Holocaust.

Spielberg would do the same with *Amistad* and the topic of American slavery, privileging the story of one specific group of would-be slaves, whose plight would encompass the horrors of slavery and the policies that the United States debated in the 1840s. No doubt that *Lincoln*, a pseudo-sequel to *Amistad*, showed that the crux of the Civil War was slavery. Spielberg's cinematic versions of these two chapters from American history (the *La Amistad* Revolt and the 13th Amendment) embody the story of the abolitionist movement.(9)

***

The Post begins with a 10 minute prologue telling the story of Daniel Ellsberg, played by Matthew Rhys. The prologue runs through his observations in Vietnam, the stealing of the Pentagon Papers and a summary of what the government report said. *The Post* doesn't need to explain the Gulf of Tonkin, the Tet Offensive, or who Hồ Chí Minh was; the tone of how the United States felt about the Vietnam War in 1971 is set from the start, and the gravitas of the situation is repeated throughout the film. The way *Schindler's List* is unmistakably a World War II film, or *Lincoln* is unmistakably a Civil War film — both without a gratuitous amount of actual warfare — *The Post* also functions as a Vietnam War film with less than two minutes of actual battle.

Spielberg's aesthetical approach to *The Post* is akin to his thrillers; there is an edge that makes this film instantly recognizable to his own *Minority Report* (2002); *War of the Worlds* (2005) and *Munich* (2005). Even John Williams' music for *The Post* occasionally parallels his score on *Minority Report* and *War of the Worlds*, yet despite the brooding tone of those other films, there is a lighter tone with *The Post*. This doesn't mean that *The Post* lacks heavy-handed moments, rather, there is a thrill to the ticking clock deadline. The development of Katherine Graham, Streep's character, takes center stage, allowing for Hanks' Ben Bradlee to be the "pirate," (as he's called at one point in the film), meant to energize the tension.

Spielberg's first film, *The Sugarland Express* (1973), highlighted the emotions caused by a media sensation, yet it was never the predominant theme of the movie. For *The Post*, Spielberg crafts a prequel to one of the most famous newspaper films, *All the President's Men* (1976). Considering how Spielberg often pays homage to his favorite movies by "winking" to them in his work (often in very subliminal ways that only hard core film aficionados will get), he channels the famous Watergate exposé to make sense of the newfound Trump era. The correlation that *The Post* makes with the actual audio of President Nixon, specifically calling for *The New York Times* to be prosecuted, is Spielberg's attempt to directly root *The Post* in the modern era.

Timing: The Women's March

The Post was released limitedly in late December 2017, and was progressively expanded into wide release by mid-January 2018. The debut of the film at the tail end of 2017 was a poetic conclusion to two major international events that took place in 2017: the Women's March and the #MeToo movement. (We'll discuss #MeToo in other chapters, although it's worth noting that a key aspect in the marketing of *The Post* was the involvement of women throughout the production.)

The subject of women empowerment has remained a key theme throughout Hollywood, yet with respects to *The Post*, the production was underway in the wake of the first Women's March, which was held in cities around the world in January 2017. Regardless of what the Women's March Organization claims to be as of this writing, the operation began the very day after the 2016 election, calling for women to march on Washington D.C. one day after Trump's inauguration. Although the organizers said they were not targeting Trump specifically and wanted the marches to be centered on women's rights — the Women's March(s) were inevitably a rally for non-Trump voters.

The Post makes very subtle, yet very obvious nods towards what Katherine Graham's legacy means in the current era. Each moment is a marvelous example of mise-en-scene "show, don't tell" cinema. Early in the film, when Streep enters a board room for discussing the final details in taking her newspaper public on the stock market, she is the only woman walking into a room packed with men in dark suits. During that meeting, she's unable to articulate herself, and the chairman of *The Washington Post* speaks for her, indicating that she actually *needs* a man to speak for her.(10) In subsequent scenes, the mere presence of Bradley Whitford's character reinforces this concept through his smug and condescending aura.

The second and more obvious correlation to the Women's March is a single shot that lasts 17 seconds. Upon Streep's entering into the American Stock Exchange to formally take *The Washington Post* public, she walks up a warmly lit (red hue) staircase for about eight seconds. As Streep ascends, she's flanked by about 18 women standing outside of the large double doors. There is really no practical purpose for these women's brief cameos except for posterity — signaling Kay Graham as a trailblazer. As the camera continues to follow Graham/Streep through the double doors, she enters into a cooly lit (blue hue) room, filled with twice as many men in dark suits.

A recurrent visual theme throughout *The Post* is the usage of darkness and light within the color spectrum of blue. As the media is a 24-hour news cycle, *The Post* therefore jumps between night and day. By the 90-minute mark of the film, the moment that Streep finally pushes back against the critics; she and Tom Hanks are the only two in bright colors as opposed to the dark suits in the room. It is the defining moment of *The Post*; Streep's character arc is complete. Her gentle and silent "However, umm" evokes the viewer's spirit, as we see her at last conjure the determination to make executive decisions on her own.

The most clear nod towards the Women's March comes at the finale, following the Supreme Court's hearing of the newspaper's case. Upon exiting, a quick exchange takes place if *The Washington Post* should make a statement to the collective media, yet Streep dismisses the offer, saying "I believe everything we've had to say we've already said." This time, as Streep descends the stairs, she is flanked by over thirty women, the majority of them younger than in the previous panning shot. The implications of this framing are the most obvious; given the political and social climate of the 2016 and 2017 era, Kay Graham is displayed as a leader for other women to look towards. Had the Women's March not taken place earlier in the year, it seems unlikely that the shot of Streep exiting the Supreme Court would be staged the way it was.

Does *The Post* Anticipate Impeachment?

Some of Spielberg's films have ironically (if not incredibly), proven to be years ahead of themselves in one way or another. The patriotic *Saving Private Ryan* (1998) was released a few years shy of 9/11 and the subsequent wars in Afghanistan and Iraq. It took ten years for the science fiction *Minority Report* (2002) to have an oddly contemporary tone given the plight of Edward Snowden. *Bridge of Spies* (2015), a story highlighting tensions between the U.S. and Russia, was released just as Russian hackers were plotting to get inside the servers of the DNC, kicking off another spy vs. spy scenario. Arguably, the most bizarrely accurate of all, *The Terminal* (2004) looks like it was custom-made for the Trump era on multiple levels.

Regardless of how one voted in 2016, Trump's victory was a surprise to the majority of the country. The shock undoubtedly fueled the Democrats' scrutinization of the election through the Russian probe and the avalanche of subpoenas. Impeachment would not become mainstream until 2019, yet it always lingered in the political lexicon throughout Trump's first term in credit to Robert Mueller's investigation. Even some Democrats campaigned on impeaching Trump in the 2018 midterm elections.

The word "impeach" isn't spoken in *The Post* (the word can be briefly seen in the background on a sign during a protest), and yet the threat of impeachment lingers throughout the film as the viewer assumingly knows what happened to President Nixon.* Nevertheless, unlike Nixon, Trump was only impeached in the House, but acquitted in the Senate; as of this writing and pending a second term, Trump appears likely to remain in office.

**

The one factoid that *The Post* accurately predicted arrives in the final scene of the film when playing the actual audio of President Nixon demanding *The Washington Post* be barred from the White House:

> I want it clearly understood that from now on, never, no reporter from *The Washington Post* is ever to be in the White House. Is that clear? … No reporter from *The Washington Post* is ever to be in the White House again, and no photographer either. No photographer, is that clear? None ever to be in. Now that is a total order and if necessary I'll fire you. You understand?

Less than a year later, the Trump administration would make a similar demand of CNN with regards to their chief White House correspondent, Jim Acosta. During a press conference in November 2018, Acosta and Trump engaged in a tête-à-tête, which grew awkward when Acosta refused to give up the microphone, deflecting an intern attempting to take the microphone from him. Other journalists joined in the fray to defending Acosta. A few hours

---

*Technically, President Nixon was never impeached. Once there was proof of a cover-up via audio tapes, the House Judiciary Committee voted to approve articles of impeachment. Senior Republicans from Capitol Hill met with President Nixon to inform him that he was most assuredly going to be impeached in **both** the House and the Senate. The following evening, President Nixon announced he would resign from office.

later, the Secret Service confiscated Acosta's press pass and barred him from the White House.

The following week, CNN and Acosta jointly filed suit against Trump and specific members of the administration for removing Acosta's press pass. *CNN v. Trump* was heard mid-November with the judge ordering that Acosta's press pass be restored for 14 days, stating that Acosta was deprived of Fifth Amendment rights and specifying that he was not being given prior notice (i.e. a warning) that his pass would be revoked. After the 14-day period, the White House reluctantly let Acosta remain provided he and the other reporters obey a new set of rules.(11)

Final Verdict: A Patriotic Film About Journalism

One only needs to watch *Saving Private Ryan* or *Bridge of Spies* if questioning the patriotism of Tom Hanks and Steven Spielberg. In fact, some would argue that the popularity of *Saving Private Ryan* played a significant role in boosting the attention that Memorial and Veterans Day receive. Regardless that the film is technically historical fiction, there is a reverent tone throughout *Saving Private Ryan* for what soldiers, specifically World War II veterans, went through during wartime.

Despite the warm relationship that Hanks and Spielberg share with Bill Clinton and Barack Obama, they have only spoken disapprovingly of George W. Bush and Donald Trump. As of this writing, Spielberg has stayed reserved, and any of Hanks' comments were fair criticism, usually disapproving Trump's brazen rhetoric. It's actually unthinkable that Hanks or Spielberg would make remarks akin to Johnny Depp, Robert DeNiro, Kathy Griffin, Jimmy Kimmel, Stephen King, or Alyssa Milano. Even Meryl Streep's speech at the Golden Globes would seem out of character for what either Hanks or Spielberg might say in a public forum.

The Post celebrates journalists who do the right thing in exposing a cover-up that displays the reckless decisions involving the death of soldiers. Unlike the whistle-blower of the 2019 Ukrainian phone call (still unidentified as of this writing), whose actions were obviously politically motivated, the actions of the actual Daniel Ellsberg and *Washington Post* were intended for a greater good. Under Spielberg's direction, the actions of Ellsberg/Rhys, Bradlee/Hanks and Graham/Streep are patriotic. Their decision to print the Pentagon Papers is courageous and done so at the risk of prison. Equally fair, *The Post* includes plenty of remarks that show Bradlee's and Graham's disapproval of Nixon, admitting bias on their part.

This patriotic perspective should come as no surprise given that "a Steven Spielberg film," has never downplayed the United States.* A common theme in *Amistad*; *Lincoln*; *Bridge of Spies* and *The Post* are Americans attempting self correction; a cultural error has happened and Spielberg's heroes make an effort to change the culture for the better. From slavery (*Amistad*; *Lincoln*) to war (*Bridge of Spies*; *The Post*), the objective is peace and non-violence.

The Post makes clear that former administrations, stretching back to Truman, were complicit in undermining the escalation of Vietnam. It also pushes the journalists on an internal level, in that both Hanks/Bradlee and Streep/Graham are disappointed with their friends from past administrations, be it JFK or LBJ. History has proven to be on the side of *The Washington Post* in the early 1970s, be it the Pentagon Papers or the exposing of Watergate.

The only times where *The Post* gets a little too heavy-handed is at the end, when Streep witnesses the young woman get snapped at by her superior before the Supreme Court trial begins. Bradly Whitford's character can seem a little too condescending on a repeat viewing, yet the character is believable for an era considered sexist.

Yes, *The Post* is a liberal movie, but it's not a film that should upset conservatives (minus those looking to be upset with anything Hollywood does). Nevertheless, the film throws in a

---

*An argument could be made regarding the portrayal of the U.S. government in *Close Encounters of the Third Kind* (1977) and *1941* (1979), although, one would be hard-pressed to call either film "anti-American."

cautionary note at the very end. *The Post* is aware of the culture it's being released in, and intentionally places a "self-check" on itself in the ending. An exchange between Meryl Streep/Kay Graham and Tom Hanks/Ben Bradlee plays as such:

GRAHAM

```
You know what my husband said about
the news? He called it the first
rough draft of history. That's good,
isn't it? Oh well, we don't always
get it right, you know, we're not
always perfect, but I think that if
we just keep on it, you know? It's
the job, isn't it?
```

BRADLEE

```
Yes it is.
```

It's fair to assume that the courage of Kay Graham and Ben Bradlee had in printing the Pentagon Papers is an admirable trait that Meryl Streep and Donald Trump could agree upon.

Chapter 2
Blackkklansman
A Race War

The Charlottesville riot in August 2017 was the worst-case scenario that Trump's critics predicted, and what Trump's supporters feared. The story of Ron Stallworth, the real "Black Klansman" is too good, too important and too heroic to just be about Charlottesville, yet the final 3 minutes of Spike Lee's *Blackkklansman* was the primary "talking point" upon the summer 2018 release, and understandably so. The images are powerful and upsetting, and *Blackkklansman* carefully boils up to that fierce finale.

Lee was not wrong to connect the 1970s with the 2010s; Stallworth himself made similar accusations in the afterward of the *Blackkklansman* paperback movie tie-in reissue. Nevertheless, the Charlottesville footage overshadows a film that offers a unique commentary about police, the black power movement, identity and the will to commit violent acts. There is a richer conversation to be had on Spike Lee's *Blackkklansman* than fixating all of our attention on Charlottesville.

The Controversial Spike Lee

Lee debuted in the late 1980s, and his popularity progressively rose in the early 1990s. The filmmaker was never one to hold his tongue when it came to controversial ideas and statements regarding race, politics and the U.S. government. Throughout his over 30-year long career, Lee has remained consistent in his behavior, openly admitting to being an instigator numerous times, yet will also say that he doesn't desire to be controversial. Rather, Spike Lee is just calling it like it is.

His fellow filmmakers have not been spared: Lee went after Quentin Tarantino for the usage of "nigger" too many times in his films, particularly *Jackie Brown* (1997). Lee and Tyler Perry had an extensive feud in the late 2000s, accusing Perry's characters of being "coon-ish." Lee had words for Steven Spielberg for both *The Color Purple* (1985), denouncing the portrayal of Danny Glover's character, and later *Amistad* (1997), claiming it was "too commercial." Robert Redford's *The Legend of Bagger Vance* (2005) came under attack by Lee for having a "magical nigger" stereotype by way of Will Smith's role. Clint Eastwood wondered, "Has he [Spike Lee] ever studied the history?" after his films *Flags of Our Fathers* and *Letters from Iwo Jima* (both 2006) were lambasted by Lee for not having black soldiers. "A guy like him should shut his face" was Eastwood's final remark, to which Lee said more inflammatory statements and then backed off, (ironically Lee used Spielberg as the go-between.)

Considering that Lee didn't hesitate to make disparaging remarks about fellow filmmakers in the press — politics has been ripe for his rhetoric. Lee's disapproval of Republicans stretches back to Ronald Reagan and has been consistent throughout. Then along comes a Republican candidate who bites and has his own set of inflammatory remarks...

Spike Lee & Donald Trump

The two New Yorkers were not wholly unfamiliar with each other; pictures of Lee and Trump do exist.[1] Yet going back to 1989, Lee went on record speaking unfavorably of Trump for an advertisement he took out, calling for the death penalty of an accused group of rapists in the Central Park jogger scandal; the faux pas is still a sore issue with Trump.[*]

Since Obama's first term, Trump has been the rallying figure for strong anti-Obama sentiments. Some would argue that the infamous "birth certificate" inquiry, despite the unlikelihood of the claim, was a stunt on the part of Trump to garnish political street

---

[*]Known as "The Central Park Five," the group of teenagers were found guilty and convicted of raping a jogger in Central Park. In 2002, DNA evidence proved their innocence, and the actual rapist admitted to his crime. To date, President Trump has not apologized and deflects the question.

cred.(2) Regardless of how true, reasonable or unreasonable the whole incident was, Trump's demanding of the birth certificate infuriated Obama's supporters, of which Spike Lee was one of the strongest.

***

Here's a fun trivial twist of fate: Barack and Michelle's first movie-date was Lee's *Do the Right Thing* in the summer of 1989. Come to the fall of 2008, Lee was euphoric in Obama's predictable election. An excerpt from an interview with the director prior to the release of *Blackkklansman* notes the following:

> In a *New Yorker* profile of Lee in 2008, at the time of Obama's nomination to the Democrat ticket, he declared that their progress was "ordained - it's providence. I think this is going to be such a pivotal moment in history" he said, "that you can measure time by BB, Before Barack, and AB, After Barack." When I quote that to him [Lee] now, he rocks back in his seat, and lets out a roar.

> "I was wrong about that! Though in one way it's true that Agent Orange [Trump] - his only agenda is to dismantle everything Obama did. I think it goes back to that correspondents' dinner when he sat there in the audience and President Obama tore him another anus. After that, as soon as he put his right hand on that lying Bible, he was getting rid of everything that Obama had done."(3)

Racially Charged Cinema

The African American culture, race and history are the predominant themes in Lee's films and the subject is addressed in a wide variety of genres. Throughout his career, Lee has remained relentless and abrasive in his style no matter how different the films look "on paper." Each are unquestionably "a Spike Lee joint." Consider how different these movies sound: *Crooklyn* (1994), a light-hearted portrayal of growing up in the black community in the 1970s; *4 Little Girls* (1997), a documentary about the 16th Street

Baptist Church bombing in Birmingham, Alabama; and *Chi-Raq* (2015), a modernized version of the ancient Greek play *Lysistrata* in the most violent neighborhoods of Chicago. All three films, despite their diverse descriptions, are aesthetically akin in style and subject matter in credit to Lee's artistry.

Blackkklansman remains one of Lee's most racially charged movies, in that the film and the characters are anticipating a race war, and the historical figures presented (Stokely Carmichael and David Duke) are two aggressive ideologies poised against each other. Much like *Do the Right Thing*, the blatantly racist rhetoric heard throughout the film beckons a violent reaction to anyone hearing it, including the viewer. Unlike the riot at the end of the fictional *Do the Right Thing*, the use of the Charlottesville footage in the finale of *Blackkklansman* validates that the battle is underway. Also, like *Do the Right Thing*, (as well as some of Lee's other films), a debate is presented through a narrative that constantly juxtaposes ideas and concepts. The plot is sloppy, although it's intentional; *Blackkklansman* constantly jumps between Laura Harrier's "black power" tirades and various Klan members spewing vile racism.

Social Debates

Watching John David Washington/Ron Stallworth outfox the Ku Klux Klan is the center drama, so the audience is conditioned to be on his side (not to mention that we can safely assume *Blackkklansman*'s audience are not white supremacists). The real subtext and agendas of the film are in the subplots, as *Blackkklansman* presents the viewer with two ideological debates: the role of the police force and ethnic identity.

Are All Cops Pigs? Stallworth vs. Patrice

Blackkklansman uses the 1970s as a way to address the modern era, specifically the #BlackLivesMatter movement pushing back against police brutality. The Stokley Carmichael speech begins with reasonable ideas, but ultimately becomes a call for violence against white people. Although the speech is romanticized, with cut aways to audience members faces, soft edged in a black backdrop, the lively speech calls for blacks to rise up and fight. As the speech goes on, the film cuts back to the white cops in the car listening in through Washington/Stallworth's wired mic (notice how the two cops are cast in shadow while the heated, anti-police words are spoken). When the speech concludes with the chant of "All power to all the people," the irony is not lost on Adam Driver's character. (This speech serves another purpose later in the film with regards to David Duke).

When the black students are invited to shake hands with Carmichael, Washington/Stallworth asks him directly if he really believes a war is coming. Carmichael confirms yes. This moment is truly when the main plight of Washington/Stallworth's character is presented in the film. How does a black cop push back against a movement that seeks to destroy his profession, while at the same time, accept a movement he belongs to by his birthright. The situation is compounded in its complexity when Washington's character falls in love with Patrice, played by Laura Harrier. As the leader of the black student power movement, she won't support Washington's/Stallworth's profession in any manner.

***

On the one hand, *Blackkklansman* does not portray police in a favorable light, yet to label the film as anti-cop would be incorrect. The grand juxtaposition of the film is at play with Harrier/Patrice's argument that "all cops are pigs," and the many reinforcements and counter arguments to her opinion.

For one, *Blackkklansman* presents the viewer with the racist cop who belittles Washington/Stallworth when he's regulated to the Records Room, and later feels up Harrier/Patrice on a traffic stop. Ultimately, the Colorado Springs' Police Department does the right thing (no pun intended) and boots the racist cop off the force at the end of the film.

At the same time, Harrier's/Patrice's arguments are not unwarranted, and *Blackkklansman* validates her perspective. In the finale, Washington/Stallworth gets taken down by his fellow officers while he's undercover trying to prevent a bomb from going off. Because Washington/Stallworth is in plain clothes, the officers push him to the ground while the wife of the KKK member falsely accuses Washington/Stallworth of sexual assault. Perhaps Adam Driver's best on-screen moment in the film is when he drives up in the aftermath, gets out of the car and yells at the officers to "stand down!" In this brief moment, the more subordinate cop of the partnership comes to the rescue of someone he's grown to look up to. The relationship of Washington and Driver is the heart of the film and worth examination.

Jewish Identity: Stallworth vs. Flip

Early in the film, Adam Driver's Flip Zimmerman retorts gruffly when a fellow officer refers to his "Jewish necklace," which Driver firmly corrects as "the Star of David." He's protective of his identity, but ignores the antisemitic rhetoric of the Klan he's infiltrating.

One of the best moments in *Blackkklansman* takes place in the Records Room between Washington (Stallworth) and Driver (Flip). After Flip's ethnicity is challenged by one of the Klansmen with a lie detector test, the incident worries the Colorado Springs police force, and the two break away from the drama for a private conversation away from the excitement. Washington (Stallworth) tries to reaffirm Driver's (Flip's) commitment to the mission, but the exchange they have is much deeper than a simple disagreement in policing tactics:

INT. RECORDS ROOM
RON STALLWORTH asks the records keeper to vacate the room. Upon leaving, FLIP shuts the door.

                    FLIP
        I didn't want to say it with
        [Sergeant] Trapp, but that peckerwood
        had a gun in my face, and he was an

ass hair away from pulling the
trigger.

                    STALLWORTH
And he didn't

                      FLIP
But he could have, and then I woulda
been dead... for what? Stoppin' some
jerkoffs from playing dress up?

                    STALLWORTH
Flip, it's intel.

                      FLIP
Well, I'm not risking my life to
prevent some rednecks from lighting a
couple sticks on fire.

                    STALLWORTH
This is the job. What's your problem?

                      FLIP
That's my problem, for you it's a crusade.
For me it's a job. It's not personal, nor
should it be.

                    STALLWORTH
Why haven't you bought into this?

                      FLIP
Why should I?

                    STALLWORTH
Because you're Jewish, brother. The so-called
"Chosen People." You've been passing for a
WASP. White anglo-saxon protestant, cherry
pie, hot dog white boy.

FLIP shifts his stance, taken aback by this
challenge.

                    STALLWORTH (cont'd)
Hmm, so what's some light-skinned black
floks? Do they pass for white? Doesn't that
hatred the Klan say, doesn't that piss you
off?

                         FLIP
'Course it does.

                     STALLWORTH
Then why you acting like you ain't got skin
in the game, brother?

                         FLIP
Rookie, that's my fucking business.

                     STALLWORTH
It's our business. Now I'm going to get you
your membership card so you can go to the
cross burning and get...

FLIP begins to walk away.

                         FLIP
   Okay

                    STALLWORTH (cont'd)
...in deeper with these guys.

Still walking away, FLIP lights up a cigarette.

                    STALLWORTH (cont'd)
Right partner?

    In many ways, Washington's Stallworth represents the
black community reaching out to the fellow marginalized Jewish
people, seeking solidarity. This conversation picks up a couple of
scenes later (again, Spike Lee's jumpy editing), when Driver/Flip
admits that he didn't fully consider his Jewish identity, but now he's

"thinking about it all the time." *Blackkklansman*'s editing presents the idea that the call to action slowly builds over time.

David Duke as Donald Trump

Blackkklansman opens with a cameo of Alec Baldwin playing a fictitious doctor, adorned with Confederate imagery, claiming that whites are the superior race. The walk-on role winks at President Trump, as Baldwin famously played Trump on *Saturday Night Live*. Baldwin's opening monologue is essentially a preface for the "race war" that's touted throughout *Blackkklansman*, more than being commentary about Trump.

Before David Duke (Topher Grace) actually appears in the film, *Blackkklansman* makes a point to link Duke and Trump, by way of what appears to be a joke. A fellow officer tips off Washington/Stallworth of Duke's attempt to run for elected office, which is a clear political jab against Trump. Yet on repeat viewings, it's clearly a setup for the link made in the second half of the film; Topher Grace's David Duke is meant to carry the racism shown in the film right up to the conclusion of the Charlottesville riot.

The Donald Trump look-a-like Topher Grace works for handful of (what appear to be) political jabs, yet Spike Lee uses "David Duke" for one of the film's most intense scenes that has a lot to do with Trump. The KKK ordination is cross-cut with a telling of the lynching of Jesse Washington. The story is told by Harry Belafonte, portraying an older man who witnessed the infamous attack. The casting of Belafonte is intentional, as he's been an active participant in the Civil Rights Movement dating back to the 1960s. The sequence is chilling because it shows two sides getting hyped, crying out chants of "white power" and "black power." Additionally, as mentioned in Stallworth's book, the Klan members screen the notorious motion picture, *The Birth of a Nation*, which serves as a communal viewing experience for them, while at the same time, Belafonte speaks of the evils the epic silent film caused (more on this later).

***

Lee's intentions for *Blackkklansman* are important to keep in mind with regards to the KKK ordination sequence. Upon *Blackkklansman*'s late summer 2018 release, Lee said:

> I hope that viewers would be motivated to register to vote.

And when winning an Oscar for Best Adapted Screenplay in early 2019:

> The 2020 presidential election is around the corner. Let's all mobilize. Let's all be on the right side of history. Make the moral choice between love verses hate. Let's do the right thing!

Ergo, it's no surprise that in the second half of *Blackkklansman*, when the KKK are shown to be growing in strength, the term "America First" gets repeated regularly. The term was used by Trump's campaign and said many times by him, specifically in his inaugural address:

> From this day forward, a new vision will govern our land. From this day forward, it's going to be only America first. America first. Every decision on trade, on taxes, on immigration, on foreign affairs will be made to benefit American workers and American families.

To further tie Trump and the "Make America Great Again" movement to the Klan, in the backrooms of the KKK ordination and the luncheon following, posters for the re-election of Nixon/Agnew are clearly seen. As with *The Post*, Nixon is the president Hollywood most often pairs with Trump.

Final Verdict: Trump-Derangement Syndrome

Unlike Steven Spielberg, Spike Lee openly has an axe to grind, and his furious anger with Trump pollutes what should be a really good drama. Lee is so focused on what he sees as a terror of the modern era that it distracts from the actual story. Perhaps the greatest offense is the usage of the term "America First" in the ordination sequence, followed by how the Charlottesville footage is utilized.

A lot of the literature and talking points put forth by the current KKK (now calling themselves "The Knights Party") is very patriotic and sounds reasonable... at first. One doesn't need to read very deep into their material to find thinly veiled racist ideologies. Although the Second Klan (1915-1944) used the "America First" phrase on some material, it became so popular within Trump's movement that it beckons a "cinematic footnote." Throughout *Blackkklansman*, the audience is shown old posters, flyers, materials, historical photos, etc., but never the actual words "America First" on KKK material. In some ways, by emphasizing the KKK's faux-patriotism, an anti-American message starts to seep out of a film that should be very pro-American.

The last image of *Blackkklansman* is the United States flag displayed upside down, typically meant to be understood as a distress signal. Or perhaps, Spike Lee intended it to be a renouncement of his country, since hanging something upside down can also mean rejection? Either way, intermixing the KKK's faux-patriotism with the student activists' chants of "black power" present a very unattractive America, which distracts from the heroic accomplishments of the real Ron Stallworth.

In the book, and briefly addressed in the film, the FBI quietly contacts Stallworth when discovering that two NORAD agents (North American Aerospace Defense Command) are clandestine KKK members. Although a mere subplot in the film, it's a frightening idea when considering the consequences of having two rogue KKK members inside the country's premiere defense system. Nevertheless, Lee's version of Ron Stallworth's story places emphasis on Trump, alienating a Republican audience and borders on encouraging hate crimes against any of the 62.9 million Trump voters from 2016. Furthermore, the book was first published in the summer of 2014, a year before Trump announced his candidacy; ergo the movie didn't need the blatant inclusion of Donald Trump, via David Duke, via Charlottesville. Unfortunately, the white supremacists gave Spike Lee exactly what he wanted.

***

The usage of the Charlottesville footage is very effective, but tying it in with Trump's infamous press conference at Trump Tower is bad selective editing. The day of the riots, even while it was going on, Trump began receiving an avalanche of criticism for a variety of reasons: the "Unite the Right" rally was openly supportive of him, the Alt-Right voted for him, Trump didn't make a statement soon enough, it wasn't a statement people wanted, etc. At the infamous press conference three days after the event, the entire episode got even more heated up with his "both sides" and "very fine people" comments. Note that President Trump's condemnation of neo-Nazis and the KKK on the day of the riot, as well as at the press conference three days later, are never acknowledged in *Blackkklansman*. Furthermore, Lee only splices footage of racist KKK and neo-Nazis attacking, showing few of the counter-protestors (specifically the ANTIFA rioters) fighting back. Furthermore, even the date of the Trump Tower press conference is wrong, displaying August 12 in the corner of the screen, when the conference happened on August 15.

A Final Note: *The Birth of a Nation*

In Stallworth's book, and depicted in the movie, the 3-hour silent film, *The Birth of a Nation*, has a cult-like status within the KKK. Similar phenomenon's have happened with *The Rocky Horror Picture Show* (1975) and *The Room* (2003), where dressing up and cheering throughout the screening is part of the viewing experience, despite the audience having seen it any number of times beforehand. Nevertheless, D.W. Griffith's film did play an unfortunate role in American history due to its popularity in the mid-1910s as Belafonte indicates in his monologue.

Unfortunately, *Blackkklansman* gets history wrong. In Belafonte's monologue, he mentions that president Woodrow Wilson had *The Birth of a Nation* screened at the White House.

Then, he repeats the quote often attributed to Wilson: "History written with lighting."

Although there is no question that President Wilson was comfortable with segregation and was not a pro-black politician, the quote is believed to be false. In fact, the only proven attribute Wilson said about the screening of *The Birth of a Nation* at the White House shows up in a letter:

> I have always felt that this was a very unfortunate production and I wish most sincerely that it's production might be avoided, particularly in communities where there are so many colored people.[4]

The other aspect of this story that's wrong is that Wilson did not personally arrange for this private screening. The producers of *The Birth of a Nation* believed that showing the movie at the White House for the president would be a perfect way to drum up publicity, as the film was relatively new and not yet seen by many people. The filmmakers intentionally kept their revisionist history message a secret from Wilson's cabinet prior to the screening. Furthermore, one of the audience members at that very first White House screening said that Wilson appeared lost in thought during the screening and exited upon its completion without saying a word to anybody.[5]

In Spike Lee's defense, conservative pundit Dinesh D'Souza also made the same fraudulent claim about Wilson arranging for and speaking the "lighting" review in his book and documentary, *Hillary's America* (2016). [6]

Chapter 3
The Front Runner
Eye of the Beholder

> How did this ever happen? How did the next president of
> the United States wind up in a dark alley with three
> journalists in the middle of the night where no one knew
> what to do? It's relevant to everything that's happening in
> 2018.(1)

—— Jason Reitman, September 2018

Consider famed author Ron Chernow and his detailed
biographies on Alexander Hamilton, Ulysses S. Grant or John D.
Rockefeller. Not once in these lengthy books does Chernow "break
the fourth wall" and parallel the history to the modern era.
Nevertheless, any reader could easily take the stories documented
in his books and quickly correlate them into the modern era.

The Front Runner has the best "legs" of the films from the
Trump era as it remains opaque in its message. The movie functions
as a historical piece. There is no question that the director,
screenwriters, producers and financiers have a political agenda, but
it's a nearly perfect bipartisan "art work." A full and proper analysis
of *The Front Runner* and the fall of Gary Hart is an entire case study
unto itself; we'll only be scratching the surface here.

Being a story about a Democratic candidate, *The Front
Runner* has an agenda by default, yet we've seen the sex-scandal
scenario repeat itself dozens of times since 1987 with both
Republicans and Democrats. By remaining a factual presentation,
The Front Runner doesn't "wink" at its audience the same way
Blackkklansman does. There's no doubt that if someone wanted to
plug Bill Clinton or Donald Trump into the movie, they could with

relative ease. Nevertheless, Jason Reitman and company choose to tell the story straightforward, much like a Ron Chernow biography.

And the Oscar for Best Editing *Should* Have Gone To: Political Campaign vs. The Mainstream Media

Not to put down the nominees and winners of the various 2018 editing awards, but the balancing of emotions and tones in *The Front Runner* is perhaps the most praiseworthy aspect of the film. The first fourteen and a half minutes of *The Front Runner* conveys multiple details while unassumingly preparing the viewer for a thriller. Two conflicting opinions will battle each other out in the following acts; the struggle is not a basic good vs. evil, or man vs. beast. Rather, *The Front Runner* presents the audience with a political campaign trying to cope with the media finding and exposing an error. (One might even argue that the "error" itself is up for debate).

Each of the topics that *The Front Runner* touches on orbit around the quandary of a politician's ability to sail through the prodding of reporters. Hugh Jackman/Gary Hart might view his dilemma as perception vs. reaction; he is the candidate trying to outfox the frenzy stirred up by the media. Even Vera Farmiga's character, as Gary Hart's wife, is a victim of the media's insistent need to stick a camera lens into their private life.

Only a handful of late 1980s policies and agenda are intermittently discussed in the film itself. *The Front Runner* is more interested in challenging the viewer about principles and integrity. The audience's emotional reaction to these questions are the fuel pumping throughout the narrative and engaging the viewer. Similar to *Frost/Nixon* (2008), the audience's personal perspective and passions get challenged (or confirmed?) regarding the historical figures presented in the film, specifically President Nixon. With *The Front Runner*, the viewer's opinions are still challenged, but the audience still anticipates Hugh Jackman's/Gary Hart's fall, whereas *Frost/Nixon* takes place post-Watergate.

Make no mistake, this straightforward presentation of history was intentional on the part of the filmmakers. Jason Reitman made it clear that:

> I'm tired of films telling me how to think, and I prefer to be given that challenge as an audience member... going in, people are going to expect one kind of film. They're going to expect a salacious film, and we have to say from moment one, that's not the story we're telling here. I'm much more interested the conversation you have on the way home, when you realize the person you just watched the movie with, has a totally different perspective on Hart's [Hugh Jackman's] relevance.(2)

What Do We Care About?

There isn't a moment in *The Front Runner* that doesn't have some little gem of information for the viewer. The smallest moments and tiny nuances contribute to the film's presentation of life on the campaign trail and the aggression of journalists. The production of *The Front Runner* structured itself in a voyeuristic style, specifically meaning that the actors and background extras would all be going at once, and the camera would wander in and focus on different moments.

Before the drama begins and the "stage" is being set, there is a little moment in the offices of the *Miami Herald*, when the chief editor dismisses news about Gary Hart, and would rather get on with discussing sports. This moment is balanced out with the aggression shown in the Hart campaign and the chronic analyzing and over analyzing of every little thing having to do with Gary Hart/Hugh Jackman. The irony is that dozens of people are obsessed with getting Hart/Jackman elected and caring about seemingly petty details, yet they ignore the major character flaw that will get the media's attention. They willingly overlook the flaw because... why? It doesn't exist if you don't pay attention to it? Voters don't care about it? The further irony is that while the *Miami Herald* remains uninterested about the presidential election, J.K. Simmons, as Hart/Jackman's ruthless campaign manager, is encouraging everyone to stay focused on the big picture.

Challenging the Audience

As stated, Reitman intended to make a film that would make viewers uncomfortable with the political process. One of the most important scenes of the film takes place on the airplane when Hart/Jackman is questioned by a *Washington Post* reporter. During the interview, the plane hits turbulence, unnerving the young reporter, AJ, played by Mamoudou Athie. Hart/Jackman is able to calm the reporter down (suggesting that the turbulence is nothing frightening, simply like "driving down a country road, just hitting a few bumps"). The camera holds on Jackman, slowly pushing in, in a lowly lit environment, cinematically suggesting "heroism" without the audience quite realizing they're being cinematically manipulated into admiring Jackman. After the turbulence stops, they finish up the interview, and Jackman loans the young reporter a copy of Leo Tolstoy's *Resurrection*. The two complete a very amicable interaction.

It's certainly not the most exciting scene of the film, yet it's one of the most important for three reasons:

- It displays an act of goodwill between the reporter and the candidate, building a level of trust. Therefore, the scene becomes a symbolic bond between journalism and politics.
- In turn, the politician sees the reporter as someone doing his bidding. The candidate can use *The Washington Post* as a mouthpiece for his agenda. Jackman/Hart has no reason to be intimidated by AJ/Athie. Ergo, the politician is the dominant figure.
- To any opponent of Hart/Jackman, the scene suggests that he is a nice guy willing to help, and also a leader, essentially winning the audience over to his side.

Herein lies the brilliance of *The Front Runner*; the scene positions the audience to take Jackman's side and helps one understand how and why journalists may have been covering for (i.e helping) politicians for decades. The exchange on the airplane sets up for the implosion that's going to come.

***

The next time Hart/Jackman and AJ/Athie are together, the precedent of friendliness continues with the two of the bonding over hamburgers. Again, a brief moment in their exchange is Hart/Jackman requesting that the burger (cooked as a campaign stunt) be mentioned in the first paragraph, reinforcing that the politician(s) have command over the media. Once AJ/Athie chooses to inquire about his marital separation, the sparks fly. It's the first time in the film that the two opposing ideologies make their "opening statements" of a "debate" which plays out in the remaining hour of the film. Flanked by his media coordinator, AJ fearfully sails into unchartered territory:

INT. DINER - DAY
AJ looks down at his notepad. A series of questions have been crossed off. One word remains - "Marriage".

AJ
(visibly uncomfortable)
Can I ask you about your separation?

SWEENEY, the media coordinator looks over, concerned with the question just asked.

HART
It's a fairly common occurrence. I'd avoid it if you can.

AJ
Ummm, look, I'm not having fun asking about this, in case you were wondering.

HART

I wasn't.

                          AJ
Look --

                    HART (cont'd)
Why should anyone care? How - how is it
relevant?

                       SWEENEY
Senator...

                          AJ
Well, some people feel like it's been hard to
know you. I'm trying to help --

                    HART (cont'd)
People? Who are these "people" everyone keeps
telling me about?

                          AJ
Okay, fine, maybe some of us.

                         HART
So, reporters?

                          AJ
Some of us.

                    HART (cont'd)
Some of you who were still in high school
when I ran McGovern's campaign.

                       SWEENEY
AJ, either ask something else...

                         HART
(To SWEENEY)
No.
(To AJ)
It's not my fault you're just arriving at
the party, AJ...

AJ

Okay, so around that time, you told Gail
Sheehy you believed in "reform marriage."
What did that mean?

HART

For crying out loud. I was young and
tired and living across the country
from my wife and I made a stupid
joke. You know, this right here, is
why people don't want to be in public
life, because someone will dredge up
something you said in a moment 15
years ago and act like it somehow
encapsulates your life.

AJ

Look, hey look...

HART

I'm going to answer one more of these, and
then I'm not going to sit here anymore. We've
covered all the stuff that matters. Did
anyone ask Reagan about his marriage?

SWEENEY

Alright, let's wrap this up...

HART

(To SWEENEY)
No - no!
(To AJ)
Did you ask Carter these questions?

AJ

There've been rumors particularly about...

HART

Oh for God sake, AJ! Ask whatever it is you
came here to ask or whatever your editor told
you to ask me. This is beneath you.

                              AJ
         Okay. Do you feel like you have... a
         traditional marriage?

                             HART
         (disbelief)
         A trad --

Breaking point. HART gets up from the table.

                            SWEENEY
         Yeah, nope. That's enough. We're done
         here.

                             HART
         You want to know what I'm doing in my spare
         time, AJ? Is that it? Follow me around then.
         Put a tail on me. You'll be very bored.

AJ scribbles, head down. As SWEENEY goes to escort
HART, he pauses by AJ.

                            SWEENEY
         That was bullshit.

Jackman/Hart's arguments are valid: he admits the quote, but then calls out the media for digging up something small from years ago. Furthermore, he passive-aggressively accuses AJ of not asking scandalous or uncomfortable questions to other candidates. Ultimately, the big question Jackman/Hart poses back to AJ (i.e. the reporters, the media, the audience), is "How is it relevant?"

Once the subject is broached, *The Front Runner* in a sense is asking the question of the viewer: What are you here to see? Are we, the audience, interested in Gary Hart's private life as well? Did we want to see him win the election and change history? Do we want to see Gary Hart become the first American president from the Western territory?

It's no mistake that the scene immediately following this exchange are the reporters from the *Miami Herald* at Miami International Airport attempting to stalk two sexy women. The audience is baited into following along.

The Washington Post:
The Post vs. *The Front Runner*

Although the two narratives are fifteen years apart (Spielberg's is set in 1971 with Tom Hanks as Ben Bradlee in his early-50s, and Reitman's set in 1987 with Alfred Molina as Ben Bradlee in his mid-60s) and the portrayal of Bradlee might be different, the same principles are in effect. Molina's Bradlee is more laid back and less biting, yet he still gives insight on how politicians operated around the media. Molina/Bradlee refrences a story when President Lyndon B. Johnson asked for privacy regarding various female roommates, and admitting that he and other journalists turned a blind eye to such discretions.

Molina/Bradlee is reluctant to go down this road of salacious journalism, yet as his younger reporters point out, it's what the readers want. It makes *The Front Runner* a good companion piece to *The Post*; consider how much energy, frustration and conversation screen-time in *The Post* was made of Richard Nixon's daughter's wedding vs. Gary Hart's extramarital affair. Despite political perspectives, *The Front Runner* confirms the bias of the liberal media by how *The Washington Post* and Ben Bradlee hunt the Republican president, yet deflects for the Democratic candidate.

#MeToo and Feminism

Once Donna Rice (Sara Paxton) shows up, the film inevitably becomes part of the #MeToo conversation, even though Rice/Paxton admits they engaged in a consensual relationship. The film wisely keeps her face off-camera, keeping this girl in mystery, indicating that Donna Rice was just another hot blonde, until the media's and the campaign's attention fixated on her.

Upon being revealed to the audience, she sees J.K. Simmons as the greatest threat to her. She presumes that Simmons, as captain of the ship, thinks very little of her. Their exchange is so opaque and the acting so open-ended, that it's hard for the viewer to determine if J.K. Simmons thinks of her as small, or if he just sees her as another mess he needs to clean up. Either way, given the political climate of the late 2010s, and despite Rice's/Paxton's clear lack of political understanding, she pushes back against the dominant white male she sees Simmons to be.

Once again, *The Front Runner* challenges the audience with the use of Molly Ephraim's character, a campaign worker whose job it is to be Rice's/Paxton's temporary handler. The short relationship they have is profound: one woman is a hard worker and the other is a byproduct of wild Florida nightlife. Throughout Ephraim's conversations with Paxton/Rice, she comes to the realization that due to this tramp, a fellow woman, the direction of Gary Hart's campaign is forever changed. To take it a step further, the sad truth is that history will never remember the character played by Molly Ephraim, yet will remember Donna Rice for derailing a likely presidency.

The Front Runner carefully transitions between subtle moments and slow burns into a crescendo of excitement in the second half of the film. Rice's/Paxton's last scene — going down the escalator into a sea of reporters looking back up for help — is brilliant. We see the fury and roar of the media, then harshly cut back to the bar with Molly Ephraim alone. This is perfect editing.

J.K. Simmons appears to be the strong man, but once he realizes that Jackman/Hart will not acknowledge the danger of the extramarital affair, he essentially checks out as the dominos continue to fall. There's brevity in the simplicity of J.K. Simmons sitting on the couch, watching a baseball game when Molly Ephraim calls to check in with him. Simmons isn't outright dismissive of her as he still inquires about her state of mind, but he already knows the game is over. It's only a matter of time until the final nails are hammered into Gary Hart's/Hugh Jackman's coffin.

***

On the other hand, Vera Farminga, as Gary Hart's wife Lee, takes a backseat for most of the film. She calmly sails through the drama with confidence, and leaves Jackman/Hart isolated in the mess. Once they reconnect in the final act of the film, *The Front Runner* goes another level deeper, bringing the audience into the intimacy between the two characters that are central to the firestorm.

Farminga's/Lee Hart's exchange with her husband is really important, because it's the culmination of all the drama. It's the result of the media's behavior and the political campaign's rebuttal. Whether or not the audience feels entitled to Jackman's/Hart's private life and affairs, the carnage and toll taken on his wife is one of the most poignant observations. Just as Jackman/Hart barks at his campaign staff for their worriment about other women coming forward with stories, Vera Farminga/Lee Hart makes her way into the hotel room. The staff scatters leaving the two alone:

INT. HOTEL ROOM - DAY.

The door closes behind the exiting staff, leaving just Gary and Lee. He's sitting on the edge of the bed, unsure whether to move.

HART

I, ummm --

LEE puts down her purse and walks over to the window.

HART gets up and steps closer to her, taking a seat.

LEE

You know, I've woken the last two mornings to the sound of helicopters. They're waiting at our gates. Dozens of them. Trucks with satellites. Their garbage littered all over the place.

HART

How's Andrea?

                    LEE
     She's disappointed.

HART is sadden by this.

                    LEE (cont'd)
     Just to leave our home she had to climb in
     the back seat of one of your staffers. He
     threw an old blanket on our daughter. That's
     how she left our home. Hiding like a
     criminal. Like she should be ashamed.

                    HART
     No, these people should be ashamed, Lee. The
     public won't stand for it, it's...

                    LEE
     (staring out the window)
     Right.

                    HART
     I'm so sorry.

                    LEE
     I can imagine you are. Were you thinking of
     me when you were flirting with that girl?
     Hmm? Were you thinking of me on that boat
     when you were making her laugh in front of 50
     other people? Were you thinking of me when
     you invited her into our home?

                    HART
     Are you leaving me?

                    LEE
     Not now. Not yet. Yeah, maybe at some
     point.
     (beat)
     And that might feel like a burden,
     and it should, because you hurt me,
     and you need to feel it, you need to

```
know that. You feel it. You carry it,
so I don't have to.
```

```
                        HART
Do you think you can ever accept my apology?
```

```
LEE looks at HART with tremendous sadness.
```

Lee/Farminga need say nothing more. In the midst of the media frenzy, the stoic victim is the woman who's belittled by the scandal itself. It makes one pause and consider the figures of Jackie Kennedy, Hillary Clinton or Ashley Kavanaugh, when the "other woman" in their husbands' wide-spread sex scandal became the front-and-center attention. In the end, who gets more press?

Final Verdict: A Phenomenal Examination

Twenty or thirty years from now, *The Front Runner* will still be watched by audiences, despite the film's low popularity upon release. The movie successfully tells a cautionary tale of American history that will likely get revived in the classrooms of politics, history, law and journalism.

There's no doubt that other political scandals will occur over the coming decades. One year after the release of *The Front Runner*, in a case oddly paralleling the saga of Gary Hart, Representative Katie Hill of California resigned due to an affair with her campaign finance manager. Hill initially denied the allegations until photographic proof of the affair leaked.[3] In May 2020, reports about the wife of Illinois Governor, J.B. Pritzker ignoring the state's non-essential travel ban during the Wuhan Coronavirus pandemic, prompted questions about double standards for politicians. Governor Pritzker countered that the family of politicians was off-topic and refused to answer,[4] similar to how Gary Hart wanted his private life unexamined by journalists.

Even if the viewer genuinely likes the "Gary Hart" character that Hugh Jackman brings to life, the audience is going to side with the journalists because the thriller is a hit job; a domino effect. We, the audience, become the voyeurs and are intrigued by the scandal. It's only after the movie is over does the viewer confront the question of Hart's adultery vs. his ability to run the country.

Ergo, *The Front Runner* challenges the viewer who believes the President of the United States should be a moral leader. Do they look upon Gary Hart with disgust because he's suave in cheating on his wife? Or does the viewer forgive/dismiss Gary Hart because he's clearly capable of being a leader (per the movie's presentation of him)? Is his lack of morality justified?

***

The Front Runner has as much to do with President Trump as the viewer wants it to. It's very easy to look at Melania's nude photos, the Stormy Daniels affair, the sexist attacks made against Rosie O'Donnell and Megyn Kelly, and then look at Gary Hart and raise an eyebrow. *The Front Runner* makes a great commentary about Trump in that he regularly rejects the decency, style and candor that we see in Hugh Jackman's Gary Hart. The film would lead you to suggest that Gary Hart would never call Hillary Clinton a "nasty woman" on the debate stage.

The Front Runner asks a question of Trump supporters: is DJT's behavior acceptable? The same question can be asked to Clinton supporters.

Gary Hart's three-week-long implosion works as a litmus test for the average voter. One would be hard pressed to accuse Gary Hart of being weak, as he fights back by sticking with the principles he believes in, much like Trump. Yet, he's unable to weather the storm of being called out for an error, and the apology essentially collapses his political life. In some ways, it becomes a validation for why Trump rarely apologizes; once you open up, asking for forgiveness, you're even more vulnerable to the media's berating (see "the Central Park jogger" mentioned in the previous chapter). Nevertheless, the way in which Trump constantly pushes past scandal after scandal is something that Gary Hart might envy.

Chapter 4

Dark Waters

The Bernie Sanders Film

Q: What was the goal you had in terms of the effect this movie would have on its viewers?

A: Films have a unique impact in making people aware of certain situations in our society and my films have almost always set out to, at some level, look at the lives of people with the interest of calling into question our social expectations. How our social practices deprive people of their freedom to be themselves. To not fit into pre-existing categories. To not be stable subjects and identities. This [*Dark Waters*] fits all of that. Films don't just make social change happen. The social change has to happen by people. Films can move you and alert you and connect you, but they have to do all those things first for action to be taken, and for what they're trying to say to have an impact. (1)

— Todd Haynes, November 2019

Of all the titles featured in this compendium, *Dark Waters* is the most reflective of the liberal progressive agenda. Make no mistake, in the years of Trump's presidency, films like *The Shape of Water*, *Blackkklansman*, *Vice* and *Captain Marvel* have all maintained a "liberal agenda," but those movies weren't necessarily the blueprints of America's political left.

The "Bernie Sanders Film"

Throughout Trump's first term, Senator Bernie Sanders was always assumed to be one of the candidates that would run against him in 2020; arguably the "front runner" because of his steadfast fan base. Furthermore, due to the controversy surrounding how Bernie lost the Democratic nomination to Hillary Clinton in the summer of 2016*, it kept him a relevant figure throughout the election and subsequent years. This means that Bernie Sanders' ideology and message(s) had time to permeate within the culture, and perhaps even influence the direction of the Democratic party.

The story of *Dark Waters*, Rob Bilott and DuPont could almost be pulled from any speech or writings of Sanders'. His autobiography and policy book, *Our Revolution*, details dozens of examples of major corporations screwing over the lowest employees for their own greed. Most importantly, in *Our Revolution*, Sanders stresses over and over that "the system is rigged" against those who are most hurt by it, or towards those who try to oppose it. There's no doubt that if the Bernie Sanders campaign were to have funded and produced a movie, *Dark Waters* would have been the final product.

The connection between leading actor Mark Ruffalo and Sanders dates back to the 2016 election, including Ruffalo himself narrating half of the audiobook version of *Our Revolution*. As one of Hollywood's most progressively left celebrities, it's important to highlight that Mark Ruffalo came from a working class family in Kenosha, Wisconsin. Furthermore, in 2001 Ruffalo had a brain tumor that, once removed, gave him facial paralysis on the left side for ten months, and permanent loss of hearing in his left ear. That type of medical emergency, specifically for an up-and-coming actor, was what made Ruffalo a firm advocate of Sanders' "Medicare for All" initiative. The subject of working class families and the financial pressures of healthcare are themes embedded in *Dark Waters*. Both Anne Hathaway and Tim Robbins have been politically active for Democratic policies throughout their careers; Robbins is also a Bernie Sanders supporter. Director Todd Haynes

---

*Simply put, the Democratic National Committee (DNC), which is supposed to remain a neutral figure in the primary races, was found to be secretly working with Hillary Clinton's campaign, giving her an advantage over the other candidates. The various tactics implemented between the DNC and the Clinton campaign most effected Bernie Sanders. Some believe that if the DNC and the Clinton campaign were not working together, Bernie would have been the Democrats' 2016 presidential candidate.

has been progressive throughout his career, specifically pertaining to LGBTQ issues, (*Dark Waters* is one of the few titles in his filmography that doesn't address the subject) and, at least in the early 2010s, Haynes was getting more political in his rhetoric.(2)

Dark Waters as a Superhero Movie

It begs repeating that all mass media - movies, television shows, commercials - have the ability to play tricks on the human mind. Although it's plainly obvious to see how the story of Rob Bilott and DuPont fits the "Bernie Sanders" narrative, there is also an indirect connection with Mark Ruffalo, via the Hulk. The legal drama makes the shy and humble Rob Bilott into the equivalent of a superhero, specifically the Hulk because the mainstream audience is conditioned to link Ruffalo to the *Avengers* franchise. Determining how much of this was intentionally a parallel on the part of the production is hard to tell. Nevertheless, the connections are worth highlighting:

Ruffalo's character, Rob Bilott, follows the character arc of a superhero origin film. Consider *Spider-Man* (2002); *Batman Begins* (2005) or *Man of Steel* (2013), in that the first half of the film is the creation process; the events that take place are to accelerate the main character into the "superhero." It's usually not until the halfway point of the film that the fully formed "superhero" truly debuts in full costume with all powers and abilities intact.

Dark Waters follows the same pattern, in that a series of unexpected events propels Ruffalo/Bilott into a legal dispute with DuPont (Bill Camp/Wilbur Tennant coming into the law office with video tapes; the drive out to West Virginia; the hostile reaction of DuPont). It's not until DuPont sends over the hundred or so boxes of documents dating back thirty years that Ruffalo/Bilott starts the "learning process." The montages with the yellow Post-It notes and the struggle to discover what PFOA means in the documents is not unlike Spider-Man or Iron Man discovering and honing their abilities. It's Ruffalo's/Bilott's relentless study and research that births the lawyer in the second half of the film.

At the halfway point of *Dark Waters*, Ruffalo/Bilott wins the farmer, Bill Camp/Wilbur Tennant, his settlement with DuPont. The environmental lawyer has taken a great risk in sueing DuPont over the location of a toxic landfill, and has proven himself to be willing to fight against corruption. Yet Camp/Tennant accuses Ruffalo/Bilott of still being "one of them." The lawyer believes that fighting DuPont any further will be a waste of time, yet he understands better than anyone how deeply rooted the corruption is. Having his integrity challenged by the lowly farmer, it provokes Ruffalo/Bilott to a new level of aggression.

In the second act of the film, as Ruffalo/Bilott truly begins to go after DuPont; he's unstoppable, much like the Hulk wreaking havoc. In the Marvel comic books and movies, the Hulk causes widespread damage and destruction, so too Ruffalo/Bilott discredits DuPont and drags them through the mud. In effect, had Rob Bilott not taken on DuPont to the extent he did, the movie itself would never have existed.

***

It's nearly impossible for audiences in 2019 and 2020 to separate the image of Mark Ruffalo from the Hulk. Throughout the entirety of *Dark Waters*, a turquoise hue in the color palette remains in over 70% of the shots. It's interesting that the scene after Ruffalo/Bilott is challenged by Camp/Tennant and he finally decides to attack DuPont, he turns on an old Windows computer that reflects a green light on his face.

The dark cinematography of the film was intentional on director Todd Haynes' part. In preparation for the shoot, Haynes specifically looked at the work of cinematographer Gordon Willis, often referred to as the "prince of darkness" by many in Hollywood. Willis' minimal usage of lighting was very influential in the looks of films from the 1970s, most famously utilized in *The Godfather* trilogy. As with *The Post*, Haynes modeled the style and tone of *Dark Waters* after *All the President's Men* (also shot by Gordon Willis). The goal, as Haynes explained, was achieving:

[A] sensibility of '70s American filmmaking, where
there was a dialogue between incredibly bold and smart
cinema, and an audience that was there to receive it, and
could interpret what was being told to them, rather than
it being shoved down their throat. There was a sense of
understanding about corruption.(3)

It should be noted that the editing pace and music of *The Post* vs. *Dark Waters* give each film a very different style. The influence of Willis and *All the Presidents Men* can be seen in the camera angles and writing of both films.

***

The second half of *Dark Waters* is simply Ruffalo/Bilott tearing apart DuPont limb from limb. He finds one horrible story after another, exposing cover up after cover up and rallying colleagues to his cause. No scene in the film is more Hulk-esque than the deposition with the Chairman and Chief Executive Officer of DuPont, when Ruffalo/Bilott spends (implied) hours going through DuPont documentation, including scientific studies cautioning against the damages of Telfon and C-8.

Yet in the finale of *Dark Waters*, as happened in real life, Bilott suffers a small stroke, caused by stress. The medical crisis, hinted at periodically throughout the movie with his shaky hand, becomes the setback that appears to take out our superhero. The herculean task attempted by the lawyer, is something he cannot achieve and has to throw in the towel. Again, the movie fits the superhero character arc; the hero is seemingly defeated at the end. Bilott experiences the "all hope is lost" moment before victory.

Winning Over the Trump Supporter

Making a movie about a major corporation whose greed directly threatened the health of the people in West Virginia is ideal fodder for what the agenda-driven filmmakers intended. In the 2016 election, Trump won every single county in the state of West Virginia, totaling 68.5% of the vote (Hillary Clinton took 26.4%, and third party votes tallied 5.1%). Additionally, the character of

Wilbur Tennant dresses like the stereotypical Trump supporter, as do all the civilians in the West Virginia scenes.

This is, without a doubt, an attempt for the "Bernie Bros." to appeal to Trump's base. Should one read *Crippled America* by Donald Trump and *Our Revolution* by Bernie Sanders side by side, the content of the two books don't appear all that different (the major exception being segments devoted to climate change). Sanders and Trump both rant against the system, call out the failures of government, the shortcomings in the economy and provoke anger in the reader. Again, it's worth repeating that in the fall of 2016, Hillary Clinton had made enemies of both Trump supporters and the Bernie Bros., which gave the two factions a common enemy: the Democratic establishment. Ergo, it's really no surprise that *Dark Waters*, i.e. the "Bernie Sanders movie," takes place in Trump's assumed guaranteed-win state of 2020. The film depicts those most likely to vote for Trump as being hurt by greedy capitalism (although *Dark Waters* remains silent on the topic of socialism).

In the true story, there were 70,000 people that were represented by Rob Bilott in the class action lawsuit against DuPont, and the money won from the initial settlement was used to fund a large scale test of Bilott's clients. The film doesn't clarify that the citizens presumed to be contaminated with C-8 were from the state of West Virginia, but it's implied. Every citizen who allowed a sample of their blood to be taken for research would receive a $400 check.

As depicted in the movie, Ruffalo/Bilott arrives on the day this testing process begins and is stunned to see the large turnout. One of the most telling aspects about this scene is the way all the extras standing in line are dressed: used baseball caps and plaid fleece lined flannel shirts. When inside one of the blood buses, Bilott/Ruffalo meets a Mom with three kids. Although she and her kids are willing to go along with the test, the mother says it's unlikely the test will find anything wrong because, "DuPont's good people. You'll see," causing a worried look by Ruffalo/Bilott. Moreover, the use of costume design is at work: the Mom has a purple windbreaker over her right shoulder indicating lower-middle class.

The costume design is subtly brilliant in its simplicity. *Dark Waters* seeks to make a contrast between the posh legal atmosphere of Columbus, Ohio and the working class town of Parkersburg, West Virginia. The two opposites suggest a unity between different classes of America.[*]

Nothing would make *Dark Waters* more of a success if it was able to awaken Trump supporters (i.e. the 68.5% of Trump-voting demographic in West Virginia) to the corruption of major corporations.

The Liberal/Progressive Agenda

With the exception of the scene where a deranged cow charges Camp/Tennant, the most dramatic moments of *Dark Waters* are centered on the human condition. Once Ruffalo/Bilott realizes that the C-8 chemical is in the water, the film becomes much more than an environmental "save the trees" piece. The Telfon monologue highlights the threat to human safety and the suffering that DuPont is putting some of its employees through.

The behavior of DuPont is what pushes Ruffalo/Bilott into a long battle with a large company that dismisses the "little guy." As the determined lawyer keeps going, he's able to rally the support of fellow lawyers to his cause, particularly his boss, played by Tim Robbins (another outspoken Hollywood liberal), who gets a perfect "soapbox" moment in the film. Although Robbins functions as a sort of referee throughout *Dark Waters*, he picks up the mantle when Ruffalo/Bilott goes to war with DuPont. It's Robbins, the chief lawyer in the film, that calls out the other lawyers for playing sides, particularly to the sides offering the bigger paycheck. This is not all that different from Bernie Sanders calling out fellow politicians for placating lobbyists and special interest groups.

---

[*]Costume designer Christopher Peterson intended for Bill Camp/Wilbur Tennant's first appearance in the film to look like he was a "fish out of water."(4)

Once Ruffalo/Bilott gets into the deposition with DuPont, the humanitarian argument comes into play. He's able to showcase years of DuPont's negligence, but also clearly point out that DuPont refers to humans as "receptors" in its documentation. It's another emotional tug in *Dark Waters* that articulates how corporations are dismissive of people lower than those at the top, including their own employees.

***

Perhaps the most quintessential "Bernie Sanders" moment of the film is towards the very end outside the Benihana restaurant, in which Ruffalo/Bilott proclaims that "the system is rigged!," the same concept that the film began with through the story of Bill Camp/Wilbur Tennant. Although it would appear that the film intends to close on the message of, 'you're going to lose,' it's the final scene that capstones *Dark Waters* so well. Just before the closing credits, the audience sees Ruffalo/Bilott in court, still fighting for the rights of the people, and as the closing credits indicate, getting the desired results. *Dark Waters* concludes on the virtue of persistence: keep going, keep pushing, keep fighting the good fight and keep your chin up. It's no coincidence that the final shot of the film, and stage direction, is Ruffalo/Bilott standing for attention in the court room.

Final Verdict: The Best Movie to Explain the Left's Frustrations with Capitalism

Throughout the majority of Trump's first term, it was believed that Bernie Sanders or Elizabeth Warren were going to be his challenger(s) in the subsequent presidential election, (as of this writing, Joe Biden is the Democratic nominee). Nevertheless, a film that is perfectly cut from the cloth of the Sanders/Warren agenda remains accurately reflective of the era. Make no mistake, a very anti-Trump team was behind *Dark Waters*, yet a film like *Blackkklansman* intentionally puts Trump in its crosshairs, whereas *Dark Waters* really doesn't concern itself with Trump. It's looking to appeal to his voters for recruitment, not to lambast and start a war with, as Spike Lee seems to desire.

Above all, *Dark Waters* is both a call to action and a warning. It shows the fruits of persistence which we see in Rob Bilott's accomplishments. This is the message and the fuel that drives the Bernie Sanders and Elizabeth Warren supporters. Furthermore, the film indirectly nods to the healthcare costs that the cancer victims of DuPont will be charged, specifically the struggling farmer, Wilbur Tennant; this is hinting at the "Medicare For All" agenda.

For a film that so accurately presents the Democratic agenda and perspective of the late 2010s, *Dark Waters* is truly belonging of the Trump-era.

Chapter 5
Richard Jewell
Clint Eastwood's American Hero

Throughout the 38 feature films he's directed, there are a number of different "heroes" Clint Eastwood has put on screen (not to mention an additional 20-odd movies he's acted in). The commonality in most of them is a person being misunderstood. These characters are often masculine figures who go out of their way to set things right. Many of them are gruf, but they are dedicated to their job, and in some cases they get prosecuted for doing so. The concept is seen throughout Eastwood's work going all the way back to the westerns (*High Plains Drifter; Pale Rider*) and the police dramas (*Coogan's Bluff; Dirty Harry*).

It wasn't until the late 1980s, when Eastwood was in his late 50s, that he started doing films that were inspired by or based on true stories, yet the majority of his filmography continued to be fiction-based narratives. This means that when discussing Eastwood's "American Hero," we're looking at a theme that didn't really appear until late in his career. They are similar to the misunderstood caricature Eastwood himself portrayed over the decades, yet each of the "American Hero(es)" are true stories of everyday people propelled into colossal events, just because they were simply doing their job. The films in which the "American Hero" theme is the central drama are *Flags of our Fathers* (2006); *Changeling* (2008); *American Sniper* (2014); *Sully* (2016); *The 15:17 to Paris* (2018) and *Richard Jewell* (2019).

Each of the main characters begin their respective films as everyday people without anything that separates them from the rest of society. Even though some are portrayed by famous movie stars, there is an effort to bury these celebrities into the setting and atmosphere. The usage of the real people in *The 15:17 to Paris* or relatively "unknowns" in *Flags of our Fathers* is another way to stress the commonality of these heroes. Specifically with *Flags of our Fathers*, the six photographed soldiers just happen to casually throw a flag up (a replacement flag nonetheless). Three of the soldiers in the photograph died in battle before they were even made aware of their fame. For most, it's difficult for people think of a time in their lives when we didn't know of the famous World War II flag raising photo from Iwo Jima, or pinpoint the first moment they saw the picture. Nevertheless, the vast majority of people couldn't name a single person in that photograph.

The Eastwood American heroes regularly reject the notion of being a hero and are often troubled by their experiences. Post-traumatic stress overtakes their sleep and daily lives as in *Flags of our Fathers*; *American Sniper*; *Sully* and *Richard Jewell*. Eastwood privileges this personal struggle they have to overcome, and in some cases, displays how this extends to family. The line most often repeated is some version of, "I was just doing my job." Even *Changeling*'s Christine Collins, portrayed by Angelina Jolie, the least recognizable figure of Eastwood's "American Heroes," was merely trying to find her son. She was performing the role of any decent mother, including caring for an imposter child.

The vicious cycle presented in *Changeling*, and seen in both *Sully* and *Richard Jewell*, is the unwarranted prosecution for a good deed. Although good due-diligence is expected on the part of government authorities, the three films depict an "everyday American" becoming a victim in his or her own traumatic moment. Thanks to government (the L.A. police force in *Changeling*; the National Transportation Safety Board in *Sully* and the Federal Investigation Bureau in *Richard Jewell*), these individuals become persecuted due to an inquiry being led with an agenda. In the end, Eastwood's "American Heroes" earn even more credit by surviving, fighting and defeating a "rigged system."

Production Backstory

In February 2014, in the wake of the hit, *The Wolf of Wall Street* (2013), pre-production was announced on *The Ballad of Richard Jewell*, starring Leonardo DiCaprio and Jonah Hill of *Wolf of Wall Street* fame. The following September, screenwriter Billy Ray and director Paul Greengrass of the hit *Captain Phillips* (2013) were signed onto the project. In the following years, Greengrass dropped out and directors David O. Russell (*The Fighter; Silver Linings Playbook*) and Ezra Edelman (*O.J.: Made in America*) eyed the project, yet *The Ballad of Richard Jewell* seemed to be stuck in "turnaround" indefinitely. Eastwood showed interest years prior, but for one reason or another, the film's status remained "pre-production."

In May 2019, it was announced that Eastwood would be directing the film with Sam Rockwell in a title role, and that production would take place in Atlanta and Centennial Park where the real events took place. Given that the film sat in production limbo for a couple years, it allowed *The Ballad of Richard Jewell* to mature with the times. What was even more shocking was that by the end of that summer, Warner Bros. announced a Christmas release date.

Dropping "*The Ballad of*," the film was given healthy commercial buzz (it certainly had more publicity and hype than either *The Front Runner* or *Dark Waters*), yet still underperformed at the box office.[1] Although the film was tagged with three sources of controversy, the lackluster response is most likely because some December releases can fall short due to an oversaturation in the market, or in this case, the cineplex.

The Antithesis to *The Post*

Although the depiction and technicality of how Kathy Scruggs (Olivia Wilde) got the scoop on the FBI investigating Richard Jewell (Paul Walter Hauser) has been scrutinized by many, the fact remains that *The Atlanta Journal-Constitution* ran with a front-page story, knowing Richard Jewell was only a suspect. Additionally, Kathy Scruggs admitted to her cousin years later that the FBI prosecutor, Don Johnson, was her source for the Richard Jewell suspect story. (Don Johnson's character was renamed "Thomas Shaw" in the movie, the character played by Jon Hamm).

That the two had a sexual liaison is creative fiction: Scruggs was openly flirtatious and suggestive to police, and Johnson had extramarital affairs.(2) The movie depicts the newspaper acting with faux self-righteousness and dignity. The arrogance of the media is on full display by their rush to have an answer, or "help" as Scruggs/Wilde says. The reckless choices end up:

- Misleading the public
- Directing the efforts of the FBI away from the actual culprit
- Placing the wrong person under intense scrutiny, and in effect threaten his life.

Despite the story being set in Atlanta, (the birthplace of CNN), it's no mistake that in the middle of the incorrect narrative being spun, the film cuts to an image of "CNN Breaking News" in the middle of a crowded outdoor restaurant. The moment clearly winks to the modern audience, with "Fake News CNN" running with a false story. If the concept wasn't clear enough, the sequence concludes with Kathy Scruggs/Olivia Wilde celebrating her "big break" in the newsroom, with a standing ovation as the journalists celebrate the headline, "FBI Suspects 'Hero' Guard May Have Planted Bomb."

The newsroom presented in *Richard Jewell* contrasts the integrity on display in *The Post* (not to mention *All the President's Men*). In one tale, we see the media hold leaders accountable and summon the courage to take a risk that betters the country, specifically printing the Pentagon Papers. *The Post*'s newsroom is kinetic; the physical printing of the newspaper is masterfully shot, accompanied with John Williams' musical score. If we consider *The Front Runner*, the journalistic integrity is in the eye of the beholder. Are we rooting for the three men in the alley with Hugh Jackman/Gary Hart? Or, are we appalled by their behavior? Either way, the viewer is (assumed to be) engaged and eager, just like the reporters, to pin down the candidate.

There is no life in *Richard Jewell*'s newsroom; Olivia Wilde is the only person who brings energy into the room and it's instantly frowned upon by the other women. Her co-author and chief editor have a flare of the conniving conman caricature, who ultimately desire a good story more than accurate history. Scruggs'/Wilde's celebratory moment the day after the story breaks is eerie; the lack of music and the extended shots of her holding the paper and laughing are cinematically dry. It displays a shallowness of journalism, but also a wickedness in that their triumph will cause widespread harm, particularly to an innocent man.

Fearing Government More Than Terrorism

Once you see Paul Walter Hauser in the film, it's nearly impossible to imagine Jonah Hill, let alone anyone else, playing that role.(3) Yet the casting of Sam Rockwell is a perfect counterbalance to Paul Walter Hauser's blind trust and idiosyncrasies; the duo is akin to the partnership of Laurel & Hardy, Abott & Costello or Penn & Teller – although more serious and contentious.

The first act of the film is rather uneventful for a high-stakes drama, yet perfectly conditions the audience into seeing Hauser's/Jewell's honesty, naiveté and integrity. At the same time, Eastwood is unafraid to loiter in his films; he often plays out scenes in which the characters simply exist on screen, allowing the audience to observe. In some ways, everything the character does, particularly with regards to Paul Walter Hauser in *Richard Jewell*, is a buffer to the narrative.

Aside from the obvious "CNN Breaking News" joke, there are small peculiarities about the film that root *Richard Jewell* in the contemporary culture. The first is the emphasis on the phrase "Quid Pro Quo" when Rockwell/Bryant gives Hauser/Jewell a one-hundred dollar bill. Giving him the cash, Rockwell/Bryant explains that he doesn't want Hauser/Jewell to become a police officer who abuses his authority. The usage of the term "Quid Pro Quo" in a 2019 film (unsure if the dialogue was in the original screenplay from years prior) *instantly* recalls that same year's "Quid Pro Joe," referring to Joe Biden's admission to getting his son, Hunter, out of a lawsuit. That incident was the starting point for Trump's impeachment over yet another "Quid Pro Quo" with regards to financial aid to the Ukrainian government in investigating Hunter Biden.

The movie allows for one uninterrupted night at the Olympic Park concert which is an extended display of patriotism. Again, this is Eastwood showcasing, allowing an extra minute or two of screen time for the audience to get familiar with the atmosphere of where the bombing took place. (Another strange timely coincidence of *Richard Jewell* was the depiction of a Kenny Rogers performance in that scene; Rogers would die four months after the film was released.)[4]

One of the most contemporary concepts of the film is a small sign Rockwell/Bryant has over his shoulder in his office that reads: "I fear government more than I fear terrorism." There is no doubt that if *Richard Jewell* was made ten years ago (even five years when it first went into production), that the sign would send a bizarre message. Yet in 1996 and in 2019, the sticker is rather appropriate to some degree. Rockwell/Bryant alerts Hauser/Jewell (i.e. the audience) into the concept that the media and FBI do not have his best interest at heart. Specifically, the motives of the two organizations are selfish; the FBI just wants to look competent and the media just wants a good story. The argument subtly proposed in *Richard Jewell* is that although the Olympic Park bombing killed 2 and injured 111, the power and reach of the government through the FBI and the media has the ability to cause significantly more chaos.

It's an uncomfortable concept to preach to victims of terrorism and their families, however given the 2019 release of the film, Rockwell's/Bryant's attitude holds merit. Because production on *Richard Jewell* was delayed and then completed in six months, the filmmakers had time to digest events such as The Steele Dossier, Fusion GPS, Andrew McCabe, James Comey, Peter Strzok and The Mueller Report, each of which took place before filming began. These events give a lot of merit to the idea that Jon Hamm/Agent Shaw would act so aggressively in his pursuit of Hauser/Jewell.

***

The original title of the film, *"The Ballad of" Richard Jewell* is rather appropriate, given that it's his lawyer's job to bring Hauser/Jewell from a state of confusion and shell shock into a combative mode. The audience is conditioned to empathize with Hauser/Jewell and his mother, Kathy Bates/Bobi, yet a disconnect remains. The party of legal counsel (Rockwell/Bryant) is unable to wrap his head around the idea that his client *doesn't* share his anger and frustration with the manipulation that the FBI is doing. It's vital for all three to get on the same level for them to prove Hauser/Jewell's innocence.

After the FBI investigates the "homosexual boyfriend" angle with regards to Hauser/Jewell's friend, a tipping point is reached. Through the prompting of his lawyer and mother, the shift takes Hauser/Jewell from a defensive position to an offensive one. The film would lead the audience to believe that the FBI and the media are an incessant all-consuming animal that needs to be fed.

The Eastwood "American Hero" comes full circle in two scenes: first in a denunciation of the media on the part of Kathy Bates/Bobi Jewell. In a speech (that was good enough to convince Academy voters to give Kathy Bates an Oscar nomination for her performance), Bates/Bobi is not unlike the mother from *Changeling*, who simply strives to protect her son:

BOBI JEWELL

I am so very drained. I hope and pray to God that nobody ever has to go through this again. I do not think any of you can even begin to imagine what our lives are like. The media has portrayed my son as the person who has committed this crime. They have taken all privacy from us. They have taken all peace. They watch and photograph everything we do. Like the media, the FBI follows his [Richard's] every move and watches my home

> constantly. And why? My son - my
> son is innocent. Richard is not
> the Olympic Park bomber. Richard
> is not a murderer. He saved
> people's lives. Mr. President,
> please clear my son's name.

The film does not offer subtext to the ending of Bates/Bobi's speech, yet it's worth noting: at the time of the press conference, the Democratic National Convention had just begun in Atlanta, therefore Bill Clinton's attention was certainly on the city. One of Jewell's lawyer, (who is not depicted in the movie, as Sam Rockwell's character is a culmination of three lawyers), added the quote to Bobi Jewell's speech, pulling inspiration from Ronald Reagan's famous, "Mr. Gorbachev, tear down this wall."

What's telling about the speech, delivered to the media, is that it's the last the movie has to say about Kathy Scruggs (Olivia Wilde). The film grants Scruggs' an admittance in getting the story wrong when she discovers that the distance to the payphones, (the location of where the telephone call was placed essentially exonerated Hauser/Jewell of the crime). Wilde's/Scruggs' last moments on screen are standing at the back of the press pool during the speech, holding back tears. Some historians have pegged the Richard Jewell Olympic Park blunder as the reason for Scrugg's demise; she died five years after the incident due to an overdose of morphine (the coroner was unable to determine accidental or suicide).

***

The second "hero moment" of the film is Hauser's/Jewell's speech to Jon Hamm/Agent Shaw in the FBI deposition. Not only is Hauser's/Jewell's disapproval shown, but possibly worse, his <u>disenchantment with the modern FBI:</u>

RICHARD JEWELL
> I'mma gonna say this, if I'm going
> to say anything: I walk in here and

I look at the circle decal on your
windows there, and I'm thinkin' –
I, I use to think that federal law
enforcement was just about the
highest callin' a person could
aspire to. But I'm not sure I think
that anymore, you know, not after
all this. I did my job that night
and some people are alive because
of that. But you'd – do you think
that the next time some security
guard sees a suspicious package,
that he or she is gonna call it in?
I doubt it, you know, 'cause
they're gonna look at that and
they're gonna think, "I don't want
to be another Richard Jewell, so
I'm just gonna run." How's that
gonna make anybody any safer?

You all can keep following me
around some more, doing what you're
doing, I can stand it, but I just
know that every second you spend on
me is time you're not spending on
the real guy who did it – and it's
like what Watson said – what
happens when he – what happens when
he does it again?

So, do you have anything you wanna
charge me with?
(beat)
Can you?
(beat)
Well, I think it's time to go.

Eastwood's Center-Right Politics

Unlike Spike Lee and Steven Spielberg, Eastwood does not share a history or an acquaintance with President Trump. However, Eastwood is one of the few major Hollywood directors who has been elected to public office. Albeit it was a 2-year term as mayor of Carmel-by-the-Sea, California, one of the wealthiest and smallest cities in Monterey County, Eastwood has done more than just make political commentary. President Ronald Reagan and Eastwood shared an open friendliness in the mid-1980s. In 2001 and 2004, Eastwood was appointed to the California State Park and Recreation Commission by the governor. In 2008, Eastwood voiced his support for John McCain, citing that the Arizona Senator was a friend of his dating back to 1970s.

Yet in 2012, Eastwood's jump back into the political fray prolonged him as part of the conversation. His 1-minute-long commercial, "Half-Time in America," for Chrysler, Dodge, Jeep and Ram during the Super Bowl had a tinge of disenchantment. However, it was Eastwood's speech at the Republican National Convention that would cement him in with the GOP. Taking inspiration from the stand-up comedy of Bob Newhart, Eastwood improvised a fictitious conversation between himself and President Barack Obama, and carried the conversation into a plug for Mitt Romney's election. The speech got mixed reviews but, it overwhelmingly rallied conservatives to Eastwood due to his anti-Obama rhetoric.[*] Later in the fall, Eastwood would appear in one more pro-Romney/anti-Obama TV-spot.

Two years later, *American Sniper* became Eastwood's biggest box office success of his entire career (including if the numbers were adjusted for inflation[5]), and became yet another rallying point for conservatives. The film was considered celebratory of guns and was attacked by Democrats for celebrating war. At the same time, *American Sniper* spurred the inflammatory question of why President Obama asked that the flags be lowered to

---

[*]The irony is that eight years previous, Eastwood upset conservatives with *Million Dollar Baby* (2004), in that the movie was seen as an endorsement for euthanasia.

half-mast for Whitney Houston, but not the late Chris Kyle, the real life subject of the film? By the time of the 2016 election, Eastwood said he was voting for Trump, but it wasn't a strong endorsement; he citied Hillary Clinton carrying on Obama's policies as the main reason for his voting Republican.[7]

***

Two months after *Richard Jewell* released, Eastwood plugged then-Democratic nominee Mike Bloomberg for president.[8] Bloomberg would drop out of the race less than two weeks after Eastwood's endorsement. (As of this writing, April 2020, Eastwood has not made further commentary).

The fact that Eastwood would reverse from a Republican to a Democrat is not altogether surprising. Trump regularly attacked both John McCain and Mitt Romney, both of whom Eastwood supported. Eastwood has called himself a Libertarian on more than on occasion, and specifically referred to himself as a "social liberal" and a "fiscal conservative."[9] His time as mayor of Carmel-by-the-Sea reflects this; he emphasized the importance of small business for the town. In this light, Eastwood's endorsement of Bloomberg makes sense. With the predominantly far-left presidential candidates (Kamala Harris, Beto O'Rourke, Bernie Sanders), and a few centrists, it's no surprise that Eastwood would back a candidate that placed an emphasis on job creation, keeping local business in operation, as well as wanting clean energy and protecting a woman's right to choose.

***

Even though Eastwood does not abide with the "MAGA" group, it doesn't change the frustrations that conservatives had with Obama. When you look at the frustrations that the right had with the Obama administration, specifically with the FBI and journalism, *Richard Jewell* makes much more sense in that light.

The Obama administration was very casual in their requests to "unmask" American citizens (a process in which Fourth Amendment Rights are ignored, citing a national security emergency)[10] so they could be spied upon. As would come to light, the Obama administration "unmasked" people so liberally (no pun intended) that it clearly gave the impression that security laws were being broke. Although *Richard Jewell* the movie doesn't get into the technicalities, the FBI agents who convinced Richard Jewell to come in for a training video and waive Miranda rights were severely criticized and reprimanded. The real person, who Jon Hamm plays in the film under a different name, clearly abused his authority to make Richard Jewell out to be the bomber. That agent died in 2003.

With regards to the Obama administration and the media, conservative pundit Dr. Sebastian Gorka makes a poignant observations regarding the Obama administration:

> Often on the way to Marine One, he'll [Trump] stop before getting on the helicopter and talk for more than half an hour to the press. If you compare that to President Obama, who actually fined, prosecuted, and surveilled journalists, and imprisoned journalists' sources, you couldn't have more of a contrast between the two presidents... You will see that it was Obama who truly and systematically curtailed First Amendment rights of religion and speech. More charges were brought under the Espionage Act against journalists and their sources by Obama than by any other president.(11)

Final Verdict: The Defining Film of the Trump Era

As presumed, the predominantly liberal Hollywood wasn't going to roll out the red carpet for films that disparaged the FBI during the Trump years. The few pro-conservative films that were released throughout Trump's first term were either documentaries (*Death of a Nation*; *No Safe Spaces*) or were under advertised (*Gosnell*; *Unplanned*; *The Hunt*). Although they all turned out less than $30 million in the domestic box office, (as did many of the liberal movies), the conservative message began appearing more towards the later half of Trump's four years.

Richard Jewell is competent because Trump is left out of the movie. The story is about a man - a gun owner nonetheless - who does the right thing, but needs to come to terms with the fact that people look at him differently <u>because</u> of his character traits, like owning guns and his emphasis on being a law-abiding citizen, albeit over the top.

Sam Rockwell's Waton Bryant might share Trump-esque opinions, but he's able to function within the movie without reminding the audience of President Trump. Unlike John Lithgow in *Beatriz At Dinner* (2017) or Topher Grace in *Blackkklansman*, who both personify Trump, Rockwell gives a much more compelling argument without dragging in a parody. Furthermore, while Rockwell/Bryant might fit the Fox News type, the performance is truly Rockwell's own.

***

With regards to *The Post* vs. *Richard Jewell*, it's worth noting that Steven Spielberg and Clint Eastwood share a history. In 2012, Spielberg said:

> I have no plans to quit. I've always said Clint Eastwood, who's one of my best friends and I've known Clint for 40 years – and we have a great, almost joking relationship about retirement. And Clint's like 81 now, and I always say, "Okay Clint, are you ready to retire this year?" and he says, "No, are you?" I say "No." I'm waiting for the phone call where Clint says he's hanging up his spurs. That's never gonna happen. If it doesn't happen for Clint, it won't happen for me.(12)

Additionally, Eastwood directed an episode of Spielberg's *Amazing Stories* television series in the 1980s, as well as *The Bridges of Madison County* (1995) and *Hereafter* (2010) for Spielberg's production company, Amblin Partners. Furthermore, Spielberg himself was a producer on *Flags of our Fathers* and *Letters from Iwo Jima* (2006) and even bowed out of directing *American Sniper*, allowing Eastwood to come in and direct it. With this in mind, both are public about which political party they support. In 2012 Spielberg donated $1 million to Obama's campaign, while Eastwood gave his "Bob Newhart-style chair" speech in support for Mitt Romney.

Ergo, while the ideologies about journalism in the two "Trump-era" films clash, neither are necessarily wrong. You would be hard pressed to call the director of *Saving Private Ryan* or the director of *American Sniper* "anti-American." The mainstream media as an organization is run by humans, and so remains capable of error as acknowledged by Meryl Streep in the tail end of *The Post*. The news media, or a documentarian for that matter, is always going to point his or her camera in the direction of the most dramatic material. This doesn't mean that all journalists, or all media people are scumbags, rather, it's simply the nature of the beast that a skewed narrative could develop. Bear in mind that although Sam Rockwell/Watson Bryant has an axe to grind with the media, he must use that same media to fight back against the FBI via a press conference with Kathy Bates/Bobi Jewell.

Dark Waters would argue that the system is rigged. *Richard Jewell* would counter that you need to use the system to fight back.

Chapter 6
The Hunt
Could This Actually Happen?

Controversial films can be tricky. Some gain notoriety for pure shock value, such as *Basic Instinct* (1992). Other titles are intentionally trying to provoke the audience by proposing contentious ideas that are meant for discussion afterwards, such as *The Birth of a Nation* (1915); *A Clockwork Orange* (1971) or *The Last Temptation of Christ* (1988). And lastly, there are movies that need to have the noise shut out in order to have an honest conversation as the folklore will distract the viewer and slant reception to the "artwork" as a whole: *Midnight Cowboy* (1969) becomes all about the MPAA rating; *The Passion of the Christ* (2004) becomes all about anti-semistim; *The Dark Knight Rises* (2012) becomes all about how Heath Ledger could have fitted into the story, not to mention a mass shooting.

The Hunt falls in all three categories. It's overtly violent for the sake of camp, it strives to be a commentary about America in the era of Trump and it garnished a lot of noise over a misperception. Therefore, we must resign to ignoring Fox News, ignoring Trump's tweet, discarding the El Paso and Dayton shootings, as well as pay no attention to George Orwell's *Animal Farm* and Richard Connell's *The Most Dangerous Game*. We must begin with the actual "art" (i.e. *The Hunt*), and then adjoin the "talking points."

What is *The Hunt*?
The Hunt is a fictionalized story, loosely inspired by Richard Connell's short story, *The Most Dangerous Game*, about a group of extensively wealthy liberals, called "elitists," who rent out a vast area of land in Croatia for illegal sporting activities. The inciting incident for this illegal game is due to leaked text messages from Athenia (Hillary Swank), a chairwoman of an unnamed

Fortune 500 company, who jokes with colleagues about killing "deplorables" in the backyard of her manor. The leaked text messages make Athenia/Swank the target of criticism from the political pundits on the right, and eventually cost Swank her ornate job. In retaliation she gathers up her liberal like-minded friends and they select twelve of their conservative critics via social media. The "deplorables" are drugged, kidnapped and flown to the rented rural area in Croatia. Upon waking up, and having no idea how they arrived there, the twelve strangers find a cache of weapons for defense, yet quickly realize they are being killed for pleasure. Nine of the "deplorables" are butchered within the first thirty minutes of *The Hunt*, and the three survivors discover the extent of the "elitists'" intention to kill them for pleasure. The silent but deadly default leader of the "deplorables," Crystal (Betty Gilpin) has the most military experience of the posse, and facilitates infiltrating the "elitists," killing them off one by one. In the finale, Crystal/Gilpin and Athenia/Swank meet, and a gory fight ensues with Crystal/Gilpin killing her hunter and walking off with her spoils.

Although the sequential plot of *The Hunt* is different from the explanation, the summation of the film is a bunch of liberals trying to kill a bunch of conservatives.

On the other hand, a more honest synopsis of *The Hunt* would be:

Crystal/Gilpin, a veteran of the National Guard, becomes the primary target of a wealthy liberal, who mistakes her for a conservative blogger by the same name. Crystal/Gilpin must infiltrate and sabotage the fake hunting grounds that has been set up for her. She uses any and all available resources to escape the death trap, and ultimately kills her captors.

In other words, it's suffice to say that *The Hunt* does not belong alongside the political dramas discussed thus far. *The Hunt* is an action flick more akin to the girls-can-kick-ass-too fodder of *G.I. Jane* (1997); *Lara Croft: Tomb Raider* (2001); *Kill Bill* (2004); *Salt* (2010), *Hanna* (2011); *The Hunger Games* (2012); *Lucy* (2014) and *Atomic Blonde* (2017). This doesn't mean that social commentary should be discarded, but rather that *The Hunt* is riding the coattails of the political climate. Even if President Trump didn't tweet about it, *The Hunt* is very much a movie of the "Trump era" and Betty Gilpin's Crystal is a role model for the late 2010s (or early 2020s).

Social Media is the Battlefield

The film is an allegory packed with allegorical annotations (references to Orwell's *Animal Farm*, Aesop's *Tortoise and the Hare*, and Alex Jones of *Info Wars*). *The Hunt* has its humorous moments, but it's ultimately crass, loud, obnoxious and vulgar... not unlike Facebook and Twitter.

The "elites" are made out to be metrosexual, petty, and self-proclaimed social justice warriors. They see themselves as rebels, taking back the country from the ill-informed by killing them. The idea of "resistance" became a popular notion among Democrats in late 2016, and reinforces *The Hunt*'s idea that liberals see themselves as the ones needing to shove off government. The few "deplorables" that *The Hunt* allows the audience to get familiar with (most are quickly killed off) are modern southern belles, working class types, or macho gun owners. Not until the end of the film is the audience shown why they are selected for the kill-fest. One of them is superimposed at the Charlottesville tiki-torch rally, another is shown with a recently killed endangered animal, and another with homophobic signs.

Therefore, while the caricatures of both the "deplorables" and "elitists" are believable, they represent an extreme view held by those on the political left and right. The film is a melting pot of modern opinions hashing it out in a physical war zone, in which the majority of the characters look like idiots. *The Hunt* stereotyping of both sides of the political argument has comical effect, such as Ethan Suplee's belief in the "Deep State" killing American citizens, or accusing darker-skinned people of being illegal aliens. On the flip side of the same coin, the "elists" quip about what's offensive in every conversation.

The gory *Hunt* is provocative in its violence. Jason Reitman's *The Front Runner* services a debate of principles, whereas *The Hunt* bypasses conversation and jumps right to the battle. The gratuitous violence in the film makes it clear that *The Hunt* is mocking the contemporary political atmosphere. *The Hunt* hints at civil war, specifically in the end (more on that later), but it's using the modern nonsensical political fighting as a vehicle for its blood bath.

The usage of text messages in the film's opening and the outcry of conservative voices and opinions on the internet is the inciting incident for the violence. In some ways the fighting like that displayed in *The Hunt* between "deplorables" and "elites," happens every day on social media. The extensive arguments on Facebook, Instagram or Twitter involve name calling, death threats and trolling (i.e. "hunting"). Users consistently say blatantly stupid things. Some will always assume the moral high ground. Others just post memes to get a rise out of their opponent(s).

Considering the fierce feminine action heroine presented in Betty Gilpin's Crystal, *The Hunt* offers a lead character who achieves victory and survival by staying above the fray. Gilpin/Crystal offers the best response to the loud (and often pointless) political fighting among American citizens. In the film, she never panics or acts in a bull-headed manner like the other "deplorables," yet is dismissive and mocking in her killing of the "elitists." Gilpin/Crystal remains the ultimate winner because she doesn't allow ideologies to distract her.

Since the audience is introduced to Gilpin/Crystal being on the side of the "deplorables," and she's the one whom the viewer is rooting for, the audience becomes conditioned to side with "right" thinking politics. Additionally, Gilpin plays the role with a southern accent and (until the twist in the final act of the film), it's never clarified whether or not she has a political axe to grind. On repeat viewing, it's clear that the "deplorables" are useless and are often the cause of their own death. Meanwhile, the "elitists" are portrayed as evil and are equally stupid because they are so rooted in their beliefs. This makes for Gilpin/Crystal to be the ideological winner.

Could It Be Civil War?

To further emphasize the intermingling of politics, the long savage fight between Betty Gilpin and Hillary Swank at the end is absurd. The stunt work and cinematography is commendable, but the tone of the scene substitutes graphic violence for gravitas. Whereas the fisticuffs in *From Russia with Love* (1963) or *The Bourne Ultimatum* (2007) are less bloody, the tension of the confrontation is dramatically stronger than what *The Hunt* offers.

The Gilpin vs. Swank fight is for shock and entertainment value; a movie like *The Hunt* needs a lengthy and preposterous brawl as it's what the buildup of the bloody gore calls for. At the same time, given that *The Hunt* is loaded with allegorical connotations, it's no mistake that they are wearing blue and red tops in a bright kitchen with flashes of white shining (American flag colors). Furthermore the colors are inverted: the presumed "deplorable" is wearing a blue top and the "elite" is wearing a red top. The two constantly jab each other, and ultimately impale against one another's body to end the row. The red and blue lay on a checkered white and black tile floor surrounded by blood and destruction making for rather obvious Civil War imagery.

Richard Connell's *The Most Dangerous Game*

In the 1924 short story, a big game hunter gets knocked off his yacht and swims to an eerie nearby island. The wayward sailor discovers a large chateau which is owned by an older and much more famous big game hunter who has secluded himself away from civilization. Over dinner the two exchange stories until the reclusive hunter admits that he's sequestered the island to himself so that he can hunt men in lue of typical wild animals. The lost hunter has become his latest prey. Over the course of a three day hunt on the island, the younger man outfoxes the seasoned veteran and kills him.

The 2020 film is a modernized and extended version of this famous short story. The manor that the "elites" hunt the "deplorables" from, and the Betty Gilpin and Hilary Swank characters, resemble the two main characters from Connell's story. Given Blumhouse Productions track record in the 2010s, specifically *Get Out* and *The Purge* franchise, *The Hunt* fits right into their filmography. Their movies place a contemporary spin on classic literary concepts.

What Went Wrong?

Obviously the production of the film was known to at least some within the Hollywood circuit. Although the majority of Blumhouse Productions features are horror, they have an impressive resume that includes *Paranormal Activity* (2009); *The Purge* (2013); *Whiplash* (2014); *Split* (2017); *Get Out* (2017) and *Blackkklansman* (2018). Even though the film primarily centers on Betty Gilpin, Wayne Duvall and Hillary Swank's characters, there were enough supporting roles of other moderately prominent actors that would have given the picture some preliminary attention. The teaser dropped July 15, 2019, which floated the idea of humans being hunted. By the end of the month, the controversy began:

- Tuesday, July 30, 2019, the official trailer for *The Hunt* drops, indicating that the plot is conservatives being hunted by liberals for sport. The film announces a late September release date. Over the next two days, the concept of the film would become a "talking point" in some political circles and social media forums.

- Saturday, August 3, around 10:45am, a far-right, white supremacist and anti-immigrant gunman walks into a Walmart in El Paso, Texas and kills 23, injuring 23. Later that evening, ESPN decides to remove all TV spots for *The Hunt* from its commercials.

- Sunday, August 4, just after 1:00am, a far-left, Antifa gunman opens fire in downtown Dayton, Ohio's nightlife district and kills 9, injuring 27.

- Tuesday, August 6, Universal decides to pull all advertising for *The Hunt* in response to the shootings.

- Friday, August 9, Donald Trump tweets the following:

  > Liberal Hollywood is Racist at the highest level, and with great Anger and Hate! They like to call themselves "Elite," but they are not Elite. In fact, it is often the people that they so strongly oppose that are actually the Elite. The movie coming out is made in order to inflame and cause chaos. They create their own violence, and then try to blame others. They are the true Racists, and are very bad for our Country![1]

- Saturday, August 10, Universal cancels the release of *The Hunt*, citing the shootings and Trump's tweet as the reasoning.

- Tuesday, February 11, 2020, Universal announces a new release date for *The Hunt* for the following month, dropping new marketing material.

- Friday, March 13, *The Hunt* finally releases and remains in theatres for just a few days. Due to the pandemic outbreak of the Wuhan Coronavirus, movie theatres across America closed their doors between March 16 and 17. Universal quickly made *The Hunt* available for streaming and digital download.

Given that the controversy surrounding *The Hunt* was the concept of conservatives being killed for being conservative, the truth of the matter was that the film *was* actually too close to reality. Some would assume that President Trump's tweet, and the noise from Republican outlets would have been the main reason to delay *The Hunt*'s release, and that Universal was using the duo shootings as a scapegoat. But truthfully, no one had seen *The Hunt* in its final form by early August (minus one test screening that caused the filmmakers to make some re-edits for reasons unrelated to current events). The fact of the matter was that in a single weekend, the United States witnessed two mass shootings; one from a self-proclaimed Trump-supporter and another from a self-proclaimed Bernie and Warren-supporter. The allegorical violence between conservatives and liberals in *The Hunt* was legitimately "too soon."

Final Verdict: Total Fantasy… Or…?

The Hunt has a problem: reality. On the one hand, the concept is so farfetched that it's unlikely to ever happen. If accusations of a political party kidnapping and torturing people in secret did appear, it would likely originate from discredited conspiracy theorists such as Alex Jones or QAnon.

On the other hand, the concept of organized killing of a group of people who think differently has happened multiple times in history. Although we haven't seen a mass incarceration of people akin to Germany in World War II or the apartheid in South Africa, political violence has spiked in recent years in the United States. *The Hunt* suffered from bad timing with regards to the El Paso and Dayton shootings, however there have still been many examples of politically charged behavior that appeared throughout Trump's first term.

- June 2017, saw the shooting of Rep. Steve Scalise from a Bernie-supporter, targeting Republicans at a practice for the Congressional Baseball Game For Charity in Alexandria, Virginia.

- August 2017 brought about the Unite the Right rally which turned into a riot. Particularly, a white supremacist drove his car into a street march, killing one in Charlottesville, Virginia.

- July 2018 had a man arrested after he was caught on video stealing a red MAGA hat and throwing a soft drink in the owner's face at a fast food restaurant in San Antonio, Texas.

- October 2018 saw bombs mailed to the homes of prominent Democrats by a loner and rampant Trump supporter, eventually arrested in Plantation, Florida.

- December 2018 produced another viral video, this time of a clerk screaming profanities because he didn't like a customer's Trump t-shirt. The employee was fired from the vape shop in Tucker, Georgia.

- January 2019 saw hundreds of threats descend on a high schooler wearing a MAGA hat in a photograph that gave the false impression that he was taunting a Native American. The teenager and his classmates were falsely condemned by the Diocese of Covington upon returning from the March for Life in Washington D.C. Video proof absolved the teens of false accusations.

- February 2019 saw a hate crime against actor Jussie Smollette actually turn out to be a staged attack, orchestrated to bring violence against Trump supporters. As of this writing, the trail is still underway in Chicago, Illinois.

At the end of the day, sipping expensive champagne and eating caviar on a private plane, or renting out a huge parcel of land in a foreign country, or playing dress up as CIA, or building a mock gasoline station for the sake of theatrics is unrealistic. *The Hunt* is beyond allegorical at that point. However, the people whose opinion and judgement of *The Hunt* would be worthwhile commentary are those who have been affected by the political violence from Trump's first term.

Chapter 7
Tapping into the Zeitgeist

All movies are worthy of extended discussion, even the ones you and I hate and think are trash. They are multi-million dollar endeavors and have something more to say than what you take away after first viewing. With that in mind, some of the films released in the last three and a half years could probably go onto becoming more historically significant to the 2017 to 2020 time frame than the previous discussed (*The Post*; *Blackkklansman*; *The Front Runner*; *Dark Waters*; *Richard Jewell*; *The Hunt*).

Each of the following tipped their hat to modern politics or, more commonly, attempted to navigate the zeitgeist of the times. They either embodied the culture of the Trump era (*Booksmart*; *Knives Out*) or offered some form of commentary about the United States (*22 July*; *On The Basis of Sex*).

Please note that I <u>do</u> enjoy some of these movies. There are even a few I enjoy more than the films we've discussed in detail. Ergo, if I appear disparaging in tone, it's only in reference to their relevance in the Trump era, not about the film as a whole.

In release date order:

Logan (2017, James Mangold) — Of all the films released during this period, *Logan* remains the most circumstantial in its parallel to the Trump era. Again, one needs to consider the release dates when looking at films, and with *Logan*'s early March premiere, and the popularity of the X-Men franchise (henceforth a guaranteed blockbuster), the movie simply did not have time to readjust itself for the obvious allegories. Regardless of Trump, the conflict on the southern border between the United States and Mexico is a subject that has made for great cinema in recent years including *Traffic* (2000); *Babel* (2006) and *Sicario* (2015). The coincidence of *Logan* being staged around children makes for an unintentional "tapping into the zeitgeist" of modern events. Even director James Mangold pointed out that he didn't think Trump would win the 2016 election,[1] yet it didn't matter to the story because the drama of Hispanic children being smuggled/used by those with malicious intentions still makes for a substantial film.

Wonder Woman (2017, Patty Jenkins) – Since the Trump era will be seen as the revival of the pro-woman movement, there is no question that *Wonder Woman* will go down as one of the defining films of the times. Unlike *Beatriz at Dinner* or *The Hunt*, which both feature heroines, the comic-book film does not make allegorical commentary about contemporary culture. Rather, it's the success of *Wonder Woman* that will be noted. Of the DC Extended Universe movies, *Wonder Woman* is considered the best of the group, both critically and commercially, becoming the third highest grossing film of 2017 in the American box office[2]. Although reactions to the DC Extended Universe movies is a very mixed bag when it comes to fans, *Wonder Woman* doesn't have any avid haters when compared to the other titles in the series. It's worth noting that the film raised the profile of two prominent women in Hollywood: director Patty Jenkins and leading star, Gal Gadot. Furthermore, Gadot was a former Israeli soldier, and given the improved relationship the United States has had with Israel, primarily because of the Trump administration,[3] *Wonder Woman* inadvertently reflects the era.

Beatriz at Dinner (2017, Miguel Arteta) — It's very important to note that the production of *Beatriz at Dinner* began filming in August 2016 and wrapped three weeks later. It premiered January 2017 at Sundance and was released in June. This being the case, *Beatriz at Dinner* belongs alongside *Battle of the Sexes* in that they both went into production prior to Trump's victory. Therefore the intended social-political commentary is potentially askew. Whereas *Battle of the Sexes* clearly anticipated Hillary Clinton's victory,

Beatriz at Dinner might have played differently if the results of the 2016 election had been different.* The film presents a hypothetical conversation between a low-income Mexican immigrant and Donald Trump (portrayed by one of the president's strongest critics, John Lithgow). The analogies are blatant: Lithgow plays a successful capitalist, a hotel owner, married to his third wife, is responsible for making life difficult for those in lower-class Mexico, and even enjoys hunting wildlife (something common among Republicans, or potentially a nod to Donald Trump Jr.). The film explores the contrast between someone who destroys life vs. someone who preserves, saves and heals. The existential ending to the film is open to translation: progressive liberals will say the finale is poignant, citing magniloquent reasons reiterating that Trump is evil(4). Moderates and conservatives will likely recognize that *Beatriz at Dinner* is aiming for some sort of cultural dialogue but will remain puzzled by the ending.

Battle of the Sexes (2017, Jonathan Dayton & Valerie Faris) — No other film feels more poised for President Hillary Clinton than the tennis drama about Bobby Riggs (Steve Carrell) and Billie Jean King (Emma Stone). The story functions perfectly as an allegory for the 2016 election with Hillary winning, given that Emma Stone's portrayal is a near-perfect caricature of a college age Hillary Rodam. Steve Carrell's tongue-in-cheek chauvinist clearly functions as the stand-in for the Donald Trump of the 1990s and 2000s, where Carrell's berating of women's liberation is more for show and shock value than it is his own beliefs. The context of *Battle of the Sexes* incorporates a LGBTQ subplot and a fight against gender inequality pay. Note that Emma Stone's character is often flanked with fellow outspoken liberal Sarah Silverman.

Avengers: Infinity War (2018, Anthony & Joe Russo) – The difference between a suspenseful and frightening villain and the lackluster "dime-a-dozen" villains seen throughout the 2010s is a

---

*We reached out for comment to the filmmakers but did not receive a response.

worthwhile debate. With this in mind, Marvel Studios found a way of making Josh Brolin's Thanos stand out: first, by periodically teasing him and then more significantly, constructing a major cliffhanger at the end of *Avengers: Infinity War*. Due to the vast popularity of the villain, Trump's critics instantly paralleled him to Thanos. This is not unlike the image of President-Elect Obama with Joker make up, a la Heath Ledger from *The Dark Knight* (2008), with the word "socialism" underneath that became popular for a brief time. Despite that Health Ledger's Joker and socialism have almost nothing in common, it was clearly latching onto the popularity of the villain of the day. The gold armored Thanos on the other hand did show a connection (which the Trump campaign would eventually play into). Josh Brolin supported the idea saying that both Thanos and Trump are "callous" in their dealing with problems, paralleling overpopulation of the universe in the Marvel movies with the difficulties at the southern border in the United States.[5]

Death of a Nation (2018, Dinesh D'Souza, Bruce Schooley) — The fourth documentary by conservative pundit Dinesh D'Souza's biennial theatrical releases about the Democratic party. A playoff of the title *The Birth of a Nation*, the film strives to make two ideological parallels: the connection between Nazi Germany's fascism and ANTIFA, arguing that the two are the same in principle. The second is the current state of America, so divided that it resembles the country during the 1860s American Civil War. *Death of a Nation* is a theoretical counter to *Blackkklansman*, addressing the subject of racism and presenting a "Republican" account of the violence akin to what was seen in Charlottesville. Perhaps the most telling aspect of the film is the interview between D'Souza and Richard Spencer in which the frailty between the white supremacist and Trump is shown. What makes this interview telling is that in early 2020, Spencer said that he, "deeply regretted voting for and promoting Donald Trump in 2016."[6]

Fahrenheit 11/9 (2018, Michael Moore) — Released at the two year mark of Trump's first term, the documentary is a shotgun blast. The film jumps between a lot of material, specifically Moore's hit job on Trump, using his own history with him and his people. The majority of the documentary is devoted to the Flint, Michigan water crisis, the DNC's sabotage of Bernie Sanders, underpaid teachers in West Virginia and the Parkland shooting. On the one hand, Moore's outrage is exhausting to the point of wondering how the man sleeps at night with so much frustration churning inside of him. On the other hand, the film does a nice job recapping aspects of 2017 and 2018, making an accurate timestamp of the era.

22 July (2018, Paul Greengrass) — Although from England, Greengrass has given the United States a few of its touchstone dramas of modern conflict, specifically *United 93* (2006); *Green Zone* (2010) and *Captain Phillips* (2013), as well as helped popularize the fictional literary assassin, Jason Bourne. Based off Åsne Seierstad's book *One of Us*, the story of Anders Behring Breivik's coordinated attack on Norway tells a more global story about the rise of white supremacy. Greengrass' *22 July* would be a few months premature, as the duo Mosque shooting in Christchurch, New Zealand (March 2019) and the Walmart shooting in El Paso, Texas (August 2019) were both fueled by passions of white supremacy. Both shooters would leave manifestos, just as Breivik did. Furthermore, the massacres were linked: El Paso shooter said he was inspired by the Christchurch shooter, and the Christchurch shooter said he was inspired by the 2011 attacks in Norway.

On the Basis of Sex (2018, Mimi Leder) — The popularity of Supreme Court Justice Ruth Bader Ginsberg started to increase during the mid-2010s. How much of it was fueled by Trump's election is hard to pinpoint, however, feminists did use her as a an iconic figure as the Women's March drew support. *On the Basis of Sex* remains relevant to the era, but doesn't define the epoch the same way that *Booksmart* (2019) or *Wonder Woman* (2017) will presumably do. *On the Basis of Sex* is an allegory for the Times Up Movement (not to be confused with the #MeToo movement) which pushes back against gender inequality in the workplace. The film presents a young Ruth Bader Ginsberg (Felicity Jones) as a loving wife, mother, tenacious lawyer and advocate of Civil Rights who is faced with sexism (both explicit and passive) at every turn. The film is littered with references to the ACLU, Gloria Steinem, Dorothy Kenyon, gender discrimination, maternal discrimination and antisemitism.

Vice (2018, Adam McKay) — Given the success of McKay's *The Big Short* (2015) a film about the housing market crash, the director of raunchy comedies tried his hand again at another chapter from that decade of history. Considering how the 9/11 and Iraq War films of Kathryn Bigelow (*The Hurt Locker*; *Zero Dark Thirty*) and Paul Greengrass (*United 93*; *Green Zone*) are obviously in their style, so too does McKay bring his suave to the biography of Vice President Dick Cheney. The film does its due diligence making appropriate winks towards the modern era (such as a quick clip of Mike Pence), but on the whole *Vice* is a 9/11 & Iraq War film a la Adam McKay's style. Audiences <u>could</u> make multiple comparisons and contrasts between Christian Bale's Cheney and D.J.T., or the Bush Administration to the Trump Administration, but you don't need *Vice* to do that. The commentary *Vice* makes on the Trump-era is what the viewer wants to see or inject. Frankly, it would be a stretch as the W. Bush years were a wartime era, which doesn't apply to the handful of missile strikes and targeted high-profile assassinations in the Trump years.

Long Shot (2019, Jonathan Levine) – Written in 2016, the film was adapted to fit the era by the time it went into production. *Long Shot* dabbles in the zeitgeist of the era as more of a parody, particularly through the Fox News spin-off, Wembley News, with Andy Serkis as a clear look-a-like to Roger Ailes. It's curious to note that a film produced by Hollywood liberals (Seth Rogen regularly attacked

Trump, and screenwriter Liz Hannah who wrote *The Post*) sends a discouraging message to left-leaning politics. Seth Rogen's liberal character regularly gets emasculated by Charlize Theron's and O'Shea Jackson Jr.'s right-leaning characters.

Unplanned (2019, Cary Solomon & Chuck Konzelman) – Having abortion as the main subject of a film is arguably the best way to have a box office flop, let alone a struggle to get distribution. Even for the popular films that address abortion (*The Cider House Rules; Juno; Revolutionary Road*), the topic is a side plot of the narratives. It's telling that *Unplanned* released in the middle of the Trump Presidency, as the administration managed to become the most Pro-Life administration in the last 40 years with the appointment of conservative judges, the steps taken to defund Planned Parenthood and Trump being the first president to speak at the annual March for Life in January 2020. It's also telling that Donald Trump formally advocated for a woman's right to choose, yet changed his stance in the mid-2000s, much like the main character in *Unplanned*, a former director of a Planned Parenthood clinic who changed her stance on the issue and managed to get the clinic in Bryan, Texas to close. A further irony is the cameo of Mike Lindell of *My Pillow*, whose company grew in popularity the following year when it became one of the first to recalibrate operations and produce facemasks in the wake of the Coronavirus pandemic. The outspoken conservative Lindell would speak at the White House and become one of Trump's strongest supporters.

Avengers: Endgame (2019, Anthony & Joe Russo) – As stated previously, connecting a firm link between President Trump to Thanos is difficult, as Thanos was an established character already part of the "Marvel" narrative long before Trump even announced he was running for office. Nevertheless, in the wake of the shocking and grim prequel, *Avengers: Infinity War*, the parallels were easy to make. Eventually, Trump and his campaign decided to own up to the comparisons by superimposing Trump's face, tinted purple, onto

Thanos' face from the finale of *Avengers: Endgame*.(7) The video showed him dissolving Nancy Pelosi, Adam Schiff, Jerry Nadler, Maxine Waters and others on the same day (December 10) that the House Democrats announced two articles of impeachment. The announcement would be a low moment for any president, yet the Thanos clip indicated that Trump was still going to win re-election the following year, despite the upcoming impeachment. The mashup is bizarre in that it makes Trump play the part of a villain in the climatic scene in which the snap-to-dust-dissolvent fails and Thanos is defeated. On a separate note, *Avengers: Endgame* also gave far-left critics a reason to complain about Falcon becoming the next Captain America, in that it was somehow in bad taste, suggesting that the shift between Chris Evans (white) and Anthony Mackie (black), should have happened during Obama's administration, not Trump's.

Parasite (2019, Bong Joon-Ho) – This is one of the most noteworthy films from Trump's first term for its significance, but not for its social commentary. *Parasite* could have been made at any point in the in the last few decades, and its message about class divisions would still hold up. To understand how *Parasite* became the first non-English movie to win the Academy Award for Best Picture is in of itself a rigorous examination of that year's multiple Oscar campaigns and studies of years past. Yet there was significance that it happened during the time of an administration that Hollywood constantly declared as racist and xenophobic. Adding fuel to the fire, President Trump ridiculed the landmark achievement later that month at a Rally in Colorado, expressing frustration that the Academy would grant their highest acolyte to a country that gives him problems with trade.(8)

Booksmart (2019, Olivia Wilde) – Teenage and high school movies are fascinating in their contextuality. The 1980s offers *Risky Business* and *Sixteen Candles*; the 1990s gave us *10 Things I Hate About You* and *Election*; the 2000s, *Mean Girls* and *Superbad*. Make no mistake, one could pull another three or four titles from each decade to give a more rounded presentation of the era. We won't know what coming-of-age movies will define the 2010s for about another decade or so, however, it's safe to assume that *Booksmart* will be ranked among the more memorable. Staged around two avidly progressive high school seniors who realize they've spent the lion's share of their years buried in academia, the movie features them trying to make up for lost time on the eve of their graduation. Since the film steeps Kaitlyn Dever and Beanie Feldstein so deep into modern feminism, *Booksmart* says a lot about millennials at the end of the decade. Even more so that these are millennials who are clearly "triggered" by Trump and inspired by the Women's March and Time's Up movement, yet the film never outwardly says so by name. There is no doubt that *Booksmart* will fall alongside *Blackkklansman* and *Joker* as a defining film of the era, but the film is one that contemporary audiences will appreciate in the course of time. (Just for fun, it would be interesting to re-watch *Easy A* and *Booksmart* side by side in a couple of years just to see how the two films aged — one from the start of the decade, and one from the end).

Joker (2019, Todd Phillips) — No other film from the 2017 - 2020 timeframe penetrates the zeitgeist like *Joker*. An authentic assessment of *Joker* deserves something akin to its own booklet in the *BFI Film Classics* series, given the angles one can evaluate the movie from. American culture has maintained a fascination with Batman since the 1940s, but it began to intensify in the late 1980s, particularly because of the Joker character. Given the role that the Joker has played in the last 30-plus years, there are multiple vantage points at which one can critique 2019's *Joker*. Because the film released in the heat of Trump's presidency, it automatically calls for extra scrutiny, given the pseudo-obsession the American culture has had with this character. Co-writer and director Todd Phillips said that Trump had pushed him into doing drama, and summed up political commentary on the film saying:

Movies tend to be a mirror, they hold up a reflection of what's going on in society. And I do think sometimes when you hold that mirror up, people don't always like what they see. [*Joker* has] been this weird Rorschach test. Both sides see it as an indictment of the other side."(9)

Ergo, it's easy to see Thomas Wayne (played by Brett Cullen) as the Trump-esque figure, or potentially a Mike Bloomberg figure: a super wealthy capitalist in a major metropolitan city running for elected office to fix problems in society. The concept paralleling Trump & Bloomberg is reinforced with protestors holding signs that say "resist." Nevertheless, for a film that still vilifies Joaquin Phoenix's character, what does this film say about the presumed Batman, i.e. Thomas Wayne's son? Is *Joker* intentionally opaque in its message? Does the "beauty in the eye of the beholder" concept work in *Joker*? Joaquin Phoenix is an attractive villain (granted that most Jokers, particularly Jack Nicholson, Mark Hamill and Heath Ledger have equally been "attractive villains") - yet the film leaves us to ponder the message: do you like what Joaquin Phoenix's Joker does? Do you like what he stands for?

No Safe Spaces (2019, Justin Folk) — As opposed to *Death of a Nation* and *Fahrenheit 11/9*'s helter-skelter approach to modern events, *No Safe Spaces* fixates itself on the topic of Free Speech, specifically in the context of college campuses. In the wake of how some students have behaved in recent years (even before Trump was elected), the film privileges Adam Carolla and Dennis Prager, two intellectual radio personalities, as they assess the environment of the modern college campus. The personality of the students is put on display, painting a picture of growing civil unrest thanks to unhealthy and unproductive conversations. Perhaps most telling is the mob-mentality of the student body when agitated enough.

Knives Out (2019, Rian Johnson) — This is another example of a film "tapping into the zeitgeist," but it really doesn't gives us much commentary back. *Knives Out* certainly tips its hand towards politics, crafting itself into a "whodunnit" of the Trump-era, but the jokes and messages can get distracting. Whereas *Beatriz at Dinner* and *The Hunt* really "feel like" political commentary from the moment the movies begin, *Knives Out* periodically peppers its "winks" throughout. Setting the story around a young immigrant from Mexico with illegal family members and embedded in a wealthy family packed with malintent, easily makes for a modern mystery/thriller. The casting of Chris Evans ("Captain America") makes for interesting commentary, given his distrust of everyone and his role to play in the plot. It begs the question of what the filmmakers are saying about the United States, via Evans, and his wicked plotting… if anything at all?

Bombshell (2019, Jay Roach) — No question that this film is relevant to the era, but even if Hillary Clinton had won the election, the film would have likely remained the same. *Bombshell* is more focused on #MeToo and passive sexism in the workplace. The events depicted in the film happened before Trump was elected. The moment the #MeToo movement developed into household-name status was throughout October 2017 when the Harvey Weinstein rape accusations came forth, followed by Kevin Spacey at the end of the month. Director Jay Roach has certainly contributed to the modern political drama (i.e. his made-for-TV movies *Recount* about the 2000 election, and *Game Change* about the 2008 election), yet like most of the films on this list, *Bombshell* fits the zeitgeist of the era, but functions better without trying to parallel it to the current White House administration, or the ongoing war between Fox News and CNN. Ironically, it's Roach's made-for-TV movie, *Game Change*, released in 2012, that perfectly anticipates the rise of Donald Trump, foreshadowed in the story of Sarah Palin.

Appendix A
Supplemental Film Reading Material

For those seeking a more rigorous study, with superior books, regarding these films and their directors, I suggest these titles. In publication order:

Directed by Clint Eastwood:
Eighteen Films Analyzed
By: Laurence F. Knapp
McFarland Publishing. 1996.

Spike Lee: Interviews
Edited by: Cynthia Fuchs
University Press of Mississippi, 2002.

Clint Eastwood: Billion Dollar Man
By: Douglas Thompson
John Blake Publishing. 2005.

Citizen Spielberg
By: Lester D. Friedman
University of Illinois Press. 2006.

Empire of Dreams:
The Science Fiction & Fantasy of Steven Spielberg
By: Andrew M. Gordon
Rowman and Littlefield Publishers Inc. 2007.

Clint Eastwood and Issues of American Masculinity
By: Drucilla Cornell
Fordham University Press, 2009.

Steven Spielberg: A Biography
By: Joseph McBride
University Press of Mississippi, 1997.
Second Edition, 2011.

Clint Eastwood: Interviews
Edited by: Robert E. Kapsis & Kathie Coblentz
University Press of Mississippi, 1999.
Revised and Updated edition, 2013.

Todd Haynes: Interviews
Edited by: Julia Leyda
University Press of Mississippi, 2014.

Steven Spielberg: Interviews
Edited by: Brent Notbohm & Lester D. Friedman
University Press of Mississippi, 2000.
Revised and Updated edition, 2019.

Appendix B
Political Book References

Since the 2016 election I have developed a fascination with politics and the Trump administration. In the last three and a half years, these are the books I have read cover to cover. I included this list so that any readers who are skeptical of what I've been consuming can see my "diet" for themselves. You can find my short reviews of these books online. In publication order:

Crippled America
How to Make America Great Again
By: Donald J. Trump
Threshold Editions. November 2015.

Our Revolution
By: Bernie Sanders
Thomas Dunne Books. November 2016.

Big Agenda
President Trump's Plan to Save America
By: David Horowitz
Humaniz Books. December 2016.

What Happened
By: Hillary Rodman Clinton
Simon & Schuster. September 2017.

Unbelievable
My Front Row Seat to the Craziest Campaign in American History
By: Katy Tur
Dey Street Books. September 2017.

Hacks
The Inside Story of the Break-Ins and Breakdowns that put Donald Trump in the White House
By: Donna Brazile
Hachette Books. November 2017.

Let Trump Be Trump
The Inside Story of His Rise to the Presidency
By: Corey R. Lewandowski & David N. Bossie
Center Street. December 2017.

Fire and Fury
Inside the Trump White House
By: Michael Wolf
Henry Holt and Co. January 2018.

Trumpocracy
The Corruption of the American Republic
By: David Frum
Harper. January 2018.

Together We Rise: The Women's March
Behind the Scenes at the Protest Heard Around the World
By: Various Contributors
Dey Street Books. January 2018.

The Briefing
Politics, The Press, and the President
By: Sean Spicer
Regnery Publishing. July 2018.

Fear
Trump in the White House
By: Bob Woodward
Simon & Schuster. September 2018.

The Russia Hoax
The Illicit Scheme to Clear Hillary Clinton and Frame Donald Trump
By: Gregg Jarrett
Broadside Books. July 2018.

Full Disclosure
By: Stormy Daniels with Kevin Carr O'Leary
St. Martin's Press. October 2018.

The Mueller Report
The Final Report of the Special Council into Donald Trump, Russia and Collusion
By: Various, under the Department of Justice
Skyhorse. April 2019.

Unfreedom of the Press
By: Mark Levin
Threshold Editions. May 2019.

Siege
Trump Under Fire
By: Michael Wolf
Henry Holt and Co. June 2019.

Unmasked
Big Media's War Against Trump
By: L. Brent Bozell & Tim Graham
Humanix Books. June 2019.

The United States of Trump
How the President Really Sees America
By: Bill O'Reilly
Henry Holt and Co. September 2019.

The War for America's Soul
By: Sebastian Gorka
Regnery Publishing. October 2019.

Triggered
How the Left Thrives on Hate and Wants to Silence Us
By: Donald Trump Jr.
Center Street. December 2019.

Acknowledgements

There's one name on the cover of a book. Sometimes two, but it's deceiving either way. The truth is that there's actually a small army of people that are involved with a book, even one on the smaller end as this. With every book I've ever done there's always a few core people at the center who are, either directly or indirectly, truly responsible for the book coming to fruition. The existence of *Make Hollywood Great Again* is credited to Larry Biela, Kristine Homan and Kelly Venticinque.

During a phone call in May 2016 with Larry Biela, I said something to the effect of being disappointed with the upcoming election. Larry's enthusiasm and knowledge about the political climate and candidates started pouring in from the receiver. Larry intrigued me just enough to rekindle my political bug which had been asleep for a couple years. He'll kill me for saying this, but Larry indirectly "woke" me. If it weren't for that phone conversation four years ago, I don't think this book would have happened. More on Larry in a moment.

Kristine Homan and I were unofficial co-workers in February 2009, and when I left that office to do filmmaking in earnest in the fall of 2010, Kristine was very supportive of my movie-making and writing endeavors. Actually, "supportive" is an understatement. Kristine held the title of my "biggest fan" for a decade: she always showed up to screenings, always took an interest, always asked what I was doing next and always pushed me to go further.

With that said… I didn't think Kristine would be the person who would rejuvenate my career. In 2019, things started to go sour for me. Nothing dramatic (or so I thought), but I realized I had embedded myself in a cycle and was getting restless. As 2019 rolled along, things got progressively worse and friends were even pointing out my slow decay. I started the research process for this book in July, but my life still felt uncomfortably routine. I needed a changeup and in September, Kristine's employer hired me to work in their office! The change was like being given a new home, with adjusted hours that made writing books and producing films more feasible - not to mention a fantastically smooth running operation! A former co-worker of Kristine's and mine from a decade ago expressed jealousy at me about getting to work with Kristine Homan again. Not to rub it in… but that jealousy is warranted.

Returning to Larry, when my life started to take this exciting new turn (thanks to Kristine), Larry turned into a mentor. Very generously, Larry has given me hours of motivation pep-talks and opened my mind to new ideas. We've mastered the art of marathon-length conversations regardless of the subject. Larry's wisdom has been profound and inspirational in helping me get a richer and more positive outlook on life. Not that I've written any sort of masterpiece, but Larry is whom I hope to have made most proud of with this book.

And then… the partner in crime. I have a theory: hire people based off their work ethic, not their obvious qualifications. Kelly Venticinque will be the first to tell you that she is not the ideal person to work with on film academia. Like, at all. I mean, like, don't tell her I told you this, but we had to find a DVD player for her to use! On the other hand, Kelly *is* the ideal person to work with if you want a competent publicist and a patient listener. Next to anyone else, Kelly put in the most amount of hours working on *Make Hollywood Great Again*. This is very much her baby as it is mine.

Actually, the baby metaphor is totally inappropriate. It's only in there to make our mutual friend, Donna Simons laugh. Truth be told, Donna will probably buy 10 or 15 copies of this book, have just Kelly sign them (because why not) and then give away to liberals saying something like, "Oh look, Donald is trying to indoctrinate Hollywood now!" just to trigger them.

A very special thanks is in order to Denise Gavlak-Yemc who temporarily employed me for three weeks, and in turn unintentionally gave me every author's dream: a mini-hiatus to write. A good chunk of this book was done at her beautiful house for which I am incredibly grateful. Denise would often say, "I'm a business bitch and I ain't got time for no shit-shows." Her gung-ho attitude was certainly an asset in getting *Make Hollywood Great Again* to come together… or as she would eloquently say, "Get it right, get it tight and vote Trump."

My brother, Dan, did one of the most competent editing jobs ever on this book. I thought I was a stickler for inaccuracies, but Dan out did me, down to finding itty-bitty little mistakes such as the misplacement of a dash.

To my family and friends, whose mere existence were tremendous help in ways they probably weren't aware of: Nick Allexon, Clint Cottrell, Mary Cronin, Eric S. Cunningham, Moira Dargis, Jenny Diamico, Dr. Carole Eipers, Sara Gorman, Kellie Halkitis, the Henik family, Mike Wade Johnson of *Faux Pas Films*, Tim Jolls, Jennifer Jolls, Kathy Kaminski, Jessica Kearney, James Kim, Olia Klein, the Lechner family, Sandra Lopez, Cindy Mayo, George Mohrlien, Mary Morley, Rita Murphy, Robert Murphy, Maria Palazzo, Amy Jo Parker, Monsignor John Pollard, Mark John Puczek, the Quintero family, Siobhán Regan, Alla Royfman, Peter Salvato, Natalia Samoylova, Marla Seidell, Don Shanahan, Rev. Richard Simon, the Solmos family, Charles Tiedje, Bobby Watson, Sophia Michelle Watson, Stacy White and Natasha Zikova.

Finally, it is only proper that I thank the filmmakers, the politicians and the pundits. Without them, I wouldn't have gotten to have the fun of writing this book.

Kelly Venticinque would like to thank:

I would like to thank first and foremost Michael Jolls. He has been intriguing from the first moment I met him. Discovering his brilliance and outstanding vision for his passion in his work endeavors is admirable. Not to mention a unique sense of humor that is quite contagious at times. I was a bit apprehensive about collaborating on this book. I felt inadequate. With your continued support I took a leap of faith and realized without risk there is not reward. Failure is not an option. I know you saw the commonality of our passions, with much diplomacy. I appreciate you having me join you on this journey. Thank you again, words cannot express my gratitude for all the times you've been so gracious to me!

A special thank you to my Mother, Father and brother Dominic. My Godfather, for all your unwavering support. My Aunts and Uncles who ignite political passion in me. My Grandparents who are no longer here but continue to inspire me with their courage and strength through their stories of their life's journeys. To some of my father's friends, you've been better to me than family. You are indebted in my heart. To those unseen, God, Bobby M. and Bob U., I can always count on you. To Donna Simons who would have never let me say "no." We take the same train together, ☺. Maria Palazzo for your compassionate support. Loralee Segreti for your friendship. I could go on. Just so you know, if you're in my life, you're appreciated. I don't take your for granted. Michael Jolls, infinite gratitude to you.

Endnotes

Introduction

1. If you'll permit another example with regards to the peculiar aging of movies - and frankly, a crass one - if we consider *Air Force One* (1997), with the hijacking of an airplane, and *Armageddon* (1998) with an asteroid creating a smoldering south tower of the World Trade Center. Both films were released relatively close to the events of 9/11, giving the action movies an unusual vibe when watched in the post-9/11 era. Even though *Air Force One* and *Armageddon* don't outright reflect the 90s, the two films have come to resemble a different era in American history.
2. *The Stephen Colbert Show.* June 20, 2018.
3. Twitter, @TrumpWarRoom. December 10, 2019 at 2:05pm.
4. There is a quote attributed to Rian Johnson, the director of *Star Wars Episode VII: The Last Jedi*, which denied the connection between Supreme Leader Snoke & Donald Trump, stating that Supreme Leader Snoke was merely an "ugly mofo with questionable choices in loungewear." (Unable to pin-point exact origins of this quote).

Chapter One – *The Post*

1. This quote has been slightly abridged.
   Emanuel Levy. "*The Post*: Interview with Director Steven Spielberg." www.emanuellevy.com. November 29, 2017.
2. Following a premiere screening of *The Post*, an unidentified reporter in the audience asked Spielberg the following:
   Reporter: Can I ask, had a certain presidential election back in 2016 had gone in a different direction, would there still have been that impedance?
   Spielberg: Yes.
   Reporter: Or are the issues bigger than one president?
   Spielberg: I think the issues are much bigger than one administration. Had the election gone a different way, I would have still found a real urge to tell the story because the first thing to attracted me to The Post was Katherine Graham, her story. It was her evolution as a real person of real potential power that did not really have the facility to exercise that power because she hadn't quite found her center of gravity. She hadn't been able to find how to use her own voice. That is part of her autobiography, *My Story*, that's something that has been written about talkin' about. I knew Katherine Graham. Before the obvious comparisons between 2017 and 1971, before all of those - it was that Katheryn Graham story, and then eventually the Ben Bradley, Katherine Graham relationship that would have made a good movie whether it had been in the last election cycle, had that gone differently, or at any time.
3. Michael Schulman. *Her Again: Becoming Meryl Streep*. Harper. 2016.
4. Sergie F. Kovaleski & Fredrick Kunkle. "Northern New Jersey Draws Probers' Eyes." *The Washington Post*. September 18, 2001.
5. Trump Rally, Myrtle Beach, South Carolina. November 24, 2015

6. Golden Globe Awards. January 8, 2017.
7. @realDonaldTrump. January 9, 2017.
8. *The Post* went from pre-production (March), into production (May), into post-production (August), and finished in time to submit for most award ceremonies (October, 2017).
9. On the topic of Spielberg's films displaying a full history lesson through a single story, consider *Bridge of Spies*, in how it privileges one event in the decades long Cold War. With all the intricacies of Russian spies, American spies as well as the entanglement of governments, the film presents a full assessment of the Cold War.
10. Frederick "Fritz" Beebe, portrayed by Tracy Letts, was the chairman of the board of The Washington Post Co. A lawyer by trade, he entered the newspaper industry at age 47. He got exposure to *The Washington Post* through working for the family of Eugene Meyer, handling estate planning and corporate legal matters. When Eugene Meyer and Graham's husband died, Beebe and Kay Graham had control of the company. Graham believed that Beebe brought a "breadth of vision that included editorial as well as business judgment" to the company. He died of complications from cancer at the Columbia Presbyterian Medical Center in New York on May 1, 1973, at age 59.
    Courtney Idasteima, "*The Post*: 16 of the Film's Stars and Their Real-Life Inspirations." *The Hollywood Reporter*. December 22, 2017.
11. In the aftermath of the White House being forced to return CNN's Jim Acosta's press pass back to him, four new rules were instituted for reporters. They were, 1) Reporters will ask a single question and then will yield the floor to other journalists. 2) Follow-up questions will be permitted at the discretion of the president or other White House officials taking questions. 3) "Yielding the floor" is defined as "physically surrendering" the microphone. 4) Failure to abide by any of the rules may result in suspension or revocation of the journalist's hard pass.

Chapter Two – *Blackkklansman*

1. There are two sets of images of Spike Lee and Donald Trump. The first is dated August 2, 2012 when they attended *Mike Tyson: Undisputed Truth* at the Longacre Theatre in New York City. The second image is dated March 14, 2013 at the *New York Observer* 25th Anniversary Party at the Four Seasons Restaurant, again in New York City.
2. The following excerpt is from *The United States of Trump* by Bill O'Reilly:
    Barack Obama firmly believes Donald Trump raised the birth certificate issue because of his skin color and his father's Islamic faith. But there is some pointed evidence that this is not true. There is no question that Trump sought to diminish Obama, but he does that to all his perceived enemies, no matter what color they are. And, as stated earlier, Trump's plan was to galvanize political support among Americans who dislike President Obama be demonizing him in a very personal way.
    The birth certificate.
    Here is the backup for my assessment: If you study Donald Trump's public confrontations, they almost always devolve into personal insults:

"Crooked Hillary," "Lyin' Ted (Cruz)," "Little Marco (Rubio)," that kind of thing.

-Later-

In America today, we the people are almost numb to controversy because there's one every ten seconds. Before almost anyone, Donald Trump understood that maulers win the debate, that harsh attacks get massive attention, that incendiary rhetoric rattles opponents.

That's what was behind the Trump birth certificate offensive. Trump wanted to establish himself as an anti-Obama person quickly. He wanted to tweak the president. It had nothing to do with skin color, in my opinion.
Bill O'Reilly, *The United States of Trump: How the President Really Sees America*. Henry Holt and Company. 2019.

3. Tim Adams, "Spike Lee: 'This guy in the White House has given the green light for the Klan.'" *The Guardian*. July 29, 2018.

4. A. Scott Berg. *Wilson*. G.P. Putnam's Sons. 2013.

5. The White House screening of *The Birth of a Nation* took place on February 18, 1915 with Thomas Dixon, the author of the book *The Clansman* on which *The Birth of a Nation* was based off of, as the person who arranged the private screening. Some believe that the fake review ("History written with lighting") was actually the words of Chief Justice Edward White whom Dixon also arranged a private screening for. Ibid. (4)

6. Dinesh D'Souza. *Hillary's America: The Secret History of the Democratic Party*. Regnery Publishing. 2016.

Chapter Three – *The Front Runner*

1. Rebecca Keegan. "Hugh Jackman and Jason Reitman Tackle Politics, Sex and the Press in the Timely *The Front Runner*." *Vanity Fair*. September 1, 2018.

2. This quote has been slightly abridged.
    Joey Magidson. "Interview: Jason Reitman Chats About Making History Into Entertainment for *The Front Runner*." *Awards Circuit*. October 30, 2018.

3. Similar to Gary Hart, it took two weeks for controversy to take out Rep. Katie Hill. On October 16, 2019, the website Red State ran an article by Jennifer Van Lear that indicated Hill was "involved" with both a male and a female staffer. The article included a few pictures and screen-captures of text messages as evidence. Hill denied the allegations saying that her estranged and abusive husband (whom she was currently divorcing) was doing this to humiliate her. On October 23, House Ethics Committee announced that they would be conducting an investigation into the allegations about Hill's affair with the male staffer. Should be allegations be true, Rep. Hill would be in violation of the House Ethics Reforms, (which ironically were implemented in 2018 in response to the #MeToo movement). The same day, Hill sent out an email to her constituents admitting to the "inappropriate relationship" with a female campaign staffer before being elected representation - hence, out of the scope of the Congressional investigation. Hill promised to work with the Congressional ethics investigation regarding the allegations. The following day, October

24, The Daily Mail released a bevy of photographs of Katie Hill with various partners, some nude. On October 27, Hill announced that she would resign from Congress and accused the nude photo leak as revenge porn.
This has been abridged from "Katie Hill (politician)" on Wikipedia.
Jennifer Van Laar. "CA Rep. Katie Hill Allegedly Involved Female Staffer in 2-Yr 'Throuple' Relationship." RedState. October 18, 2019.
Josh Boswell, Martin Gould, Jennifer Van Laar. "Shocking photos of Congresswoman Katie Hill are revealed showing off Nazi-era tattoo while smoking a bong, kissing her female staffer and posing nude on 'wife sharing' sites." *The Daily Mail.* October 24, 2019.

4. During a press conference on May 1, 2020, Gov. Pritzker was asked about the location of his wife in the wake of Illinois extending the stay-at-home order pass the deadline originally given. A reporter fielding the questions asked:
"Mark Konkol with the *Patch* says, 'Where's the first lady? Is she accompanied by a state security detail? Is she engaged in non-essential travel? What is your response to people who say the stay-at-home order and non-essential travel bans aren't abided by your family?' I believe there is a report from *Illinois Rising Action* that says that she recently traveled to Florida."
"Well, first of all I'd like to say is that in politics, it used to be that we kept our families out of it. My official duties have nothing to do with my family. So, I'm just not going to answer that question. It's inappropriate and I find it reprehensible, honestly, that uha, that report wrote a story about it."
State of Illinois Coronavirus (COVID-19) Response, Daily Press Briefing. May 1, 2020.

Chapter Four – *Dark Waters*

1. Max Cea. "The Director of *Dark Waters* Promises His Movie is Actually Uplifting." *GQ*. November 22, 2019.
2. Julie Leyda, "'Something That Is Dangerous and Arousing and Transgressive': An Interview with Todd Haynes." *Bright Lights Film Journal*. November 2012.
3. This quote has been abridged.
   K. Austin Collins. "How the Cinematography of *All the President's Men* and *The Godfather* Influenced Todd Haynes' *Dark Waters*." *Vanity Fair*. November 23, 2019.
4. *Dark Waters* DVD. Special Features: "The Real People." 2020.

Chapter Five – *Richard Jewell*

1. *Richard Jewell* earned a total of $22.3 million in the domestic box office, with an additional $21.4 million in the foreign markets. Of Eastwood's directorial features, this was the lowest grossing since 1999's *True Crime*. Technically *Letters from Iwo Jima* performed the poorest in the United States box office, yet the gross in the foreign markets made up for any losses.
2. Chapter 27.

Kent Alexander & Kevin Salwen. *"The Suspect: An Olympic Bombing, The FBI, The Media, and Richard Jewell, The Man Caught in the Middle."* Abrams Press. 2019.

3. The casting of Leonardo DiCaprio as Watson Bryant, presumably under the direction of Paul Greengrass' intense aesthetic would have made for a film similar to Greengrass' own terror-courtroom drama *22 July* (2018).

4. Kenny Rogers is portrayed by Ronnie Allen in the film. Allen has been a Rogers impersonator for almost 40 years.

5. Chapter 17. Ibid. (2)

6. *American Sniper* made $350.1 million in the domestic box office, plus an additional $197.3 million in the foreign markets. No other Clint Eastwood film had brought in a box office gross of that size, even if the numbers were adjusted for inflation. *American Sniper* was the highest grossing film of 2014, although ironically, it made over 99% of its money in 2015; the film released December 25, 2014 in a very limitedly engagement and stayed that way until mid-January. The Thursday morning of the day that *American Sniper* would open "wide", it was nominated for Best Picture, and Bradley Cooper Best Actor, giving the film a boost in popularity.

7. The Hollywood Reporter Staff. "Clint Eastwood on the 'Pussy' Generation and Why He's Voting for Donald Trump." *The Hollywood Reporter*. August 3, 2016.

8. Tunku Varadarajan, "A Hollywood Legend Talks Politics." *The Wall Street Journal*. February 21, 2020.

9. *Premiere Magazine*. March 1999.

10. The following excerpt is taken from *The War For America's Soul* by Sebastian Gorka:

"When a government official makes a justifiable request to surveil a target individual, any intercepted communication that involves an American citizen who is not otherwise under investigation — who is not being surveilled as an individual of primary interest because he committed a crime or because there is reason to suspect that he will — must be handled in such a way that that individual's identity is "masked" or reduced within the intercepted material, so as to protect that U.S. citizen's constitutional rights. There is, however, an exception.

If a senior government official is curious as to why this American's name can be connected to a person deemed a threat to national security, they can be request that the person's name be revealed. This is called "unmasking" and should be invoked rarely and only if there is one valid national security justification for injuring that citizen's Fourth Amendment rights. Having spoken to senior political appointees and intelligence professional with multiple decades of government service, I was told that if you make more than a handful of unmasking requests in your entire time in government that is highly unusual.

—Later—

In the last year of the Obama administration, according to PBS, hardly a rabid rightwing source, more than 1,900 American's identities were revealed based on these previously incredibly rare requests. In just one year.

Sebastian Gorka. *The War For America's Soul*. Regnery Publishing. October 2019.

11. Ibid. (10)
12. *War Horse*, London, England premiere. Press Conference.

Chapter Six – *The Hunt*
1. Twitter, @realDonaldTrump. August 9, 2019 at 1:44pm.

Chapter Seven – Tapping into the Zeitgeist
1. Abraham Riesman, "*Logan* Director James Mangold on Trump's Influence, the Film's Last Line, and the Biggest Problem with Superhero Movies." *Vulture*. March 6, 2017.
2. *Wonder Woman* earned $412.5 million in the domestic box office, with an additional $409.2 million in the foreign markets. In the global box office it was the tenth highest grossing film of the year.
3. The two biggest events that drastically improved the United States' relationship to Israel was recognizing Jerusalem as the capital and moving the U.S. embassy to it. Secondly, was recognizing Israel's sovereignty over the Golan Heights. Additionally, Prime Minister Benjamin Netanyahu has been extremely praiseworthy of President Trump.
4. Perhaps the most "progressive" reflection on the ending to *Beatriz at Dinner* can be found at:
Stephanie Jo Kent. "Why is the Ending of *Beatriz at Dinner* so Unsettling?" *Dark Allies*. June 25, 2017
5. *The Stephen Colbert Show*. June 20, 2018.
6. Twitter, @RichardBSpencer. January 7, 2020 at 6:35pm.
7. The tweet was accompanied with: "House Democrats can push their shame impeachment all they want. President Trump's re-election is inevitable." Twitter, @TrumpWarRoom. December 10, 2019 at 2:50pm.
8. "By the way, how bad were the Academy Awards this year? Did you see them? 'And the winner is a movie from South Korea!' What the hell was that all about? We got enough problems with South Korea, with trade, on top of it they give them the best movie of the year? Was it good? I don't know. You know I'm lookin' for like, where's, let's get *Gone with the Wind*. Can we get *Gone with the Wind* back, please? *Sunset Boulevard*? So many great movies. 'The winner is, from South Korea.' I thought it was Best Foreign Film, right? 'Best Foreign Movie!' Did this ever happen before?"
Broadmoor World Arena. Colorado Springs, Co. Thursday, February 20, 2020.

Index

About the Author

Michael Jolls is the author of the book *The Films of Steven Spielberg* (2018), co-author of *Rev. William Netestraeter: A Life in Three Parts* (2019) with his brother, Daniel. He was also assistant editor on *David Fincher: Interviews* (2014).

Jolls has also been involved with over a hundred film projects ranging from comedies, to documentaries, to feature-length. His works includes *6 Rules* (2011); the *Uncle Colt & Cletus* series (2012-2014); *Cathedral of the North Shore* (2013); *The Great Chicago Filmmaker* (2015); the *#SelfieGuy* series (2015-2017); *Sell Me This Pen* (2018) and *A Sad State of Affairs* (2020).

Made in the USA
Middletown, DE
17 July 2022